125th

Anniversary PRAYER

Lord, 125 years ago
Holy Cross Cemetery was placed
Under the sign of the cross, to be,
By the power of your blessing,
A place of rest and hope.

May the bodies buried here
sleep in your peace,
to rise immortal
at the coming of your Son.

May this place continue
to be a comfort to the living -
a sign of hope
for their unending life.

For centuries to come,
may prayer be continually offered here
for those who sleep in Christ
and in constant praise
of your mercy.

We ask this through
Christ our Lord. Amen.

In 1868, the San Francisco-San Jose railroad line joined the Southern Pacific Railroad and became part of California's statewide system.

In this photo, Southern Pacific Locomotive 2375 arrives at the Holy Cross Gateway and Lodge Building, also known as McMahon Station. Designed by Frank T. Shea and William D. Shea in 1902, the building served as an office for the Cemetery as well as a station for funeral parties and visitors. Its wide doorway was built to accommodate a casket coming off the train. The building, not currently in use, is considered an excellent example of what is known as the Richardson Romanesque architectural style.

HOLY CROSS CATHOLIC CEMETERY ~ COLMA

125 Years of
HISTORY, MINISTRY & SERVICE

Written by Jean Bartlett

Jean Bartlett photo

"All things have their season, and in their times
all things pass under heaven;
a time to be born and a time to die…" (Eccl. 3:1-11)

Printed in San Mateo, California

PRINT COPY XPRESS
T: (650) 356-0152 | F: (650) 356-0231 | www.pcxusa.net
2012

Jean Bartlett photo

*Statute of Jesus at the funeral
entrance on "Old" Mission Road*

*"Come to Me, all you who labour,
and are burdened, and I will give you rest."
(Matt. 11:28)*

ISBN 978-0-9859424-0-3

Printed in San Mateo, California
By Print Copy Xpress

Book jacket art © 2012 by Hugh Zeng*
(*379 El Camino Real, Millbrae)

Table OF CONTENTS

MT. REV. J. S. ALEMANY, O. S. D.,
FIRST ARCH-BISHOP OF S. F.

Archbishop Joseph Sadoc Alemany, first Archbishop of San Francisco (1853-1884)

The Establishment of the

ROMAN CATHOLIC
ARCHDIOCESE OF SAN FRANCISCO

On June 16, 1846, Cardinal Giovanni Mastai-Ferretti was elected to the papacy as Pope Pius IX. Serving as head of the Roman Catholic Church from 1846-1878, his pontificate is the longest in history. During his reign, the Catholic population in the United States increased from four percent in 1846 to eleven percent in 1878. In addition, the number of priests serving the Roman Catholic citizens of this relatively new country grew from 700 in 1846 to 6,000 in 1878.

Considered the father of the modern American Catholic Church, Pope Pius IX created many of the U.S. dioceses and archdioceses including Albany, Cleveland, Monterey, Savannah, St. Paul, Santa Fe, Covington, Harrisburg, Columbus and Galveston-Houston. On July 29, 1853, Pope Pius IX established the Roman Catholic Archdiocese of San Francisco and named Joseph Sadoc Alemany the City's first Archbishop (1853-1884). The Archdiocese extended north to the Oregon-California border, east to the Colorado River in Colorado and south to the Diocese of Monterey.

San Francisco's first Archbishop was born in Spain in 1814 and entered the Dominican Order in 1830. In 1837, Alemany was ordained a priest, and in 1840, the Dominicans sent him to the United States where he worked as a missionary in Kentucky, Ohio and Tennessee. He also became a naturalized American citizen. Beginning in 1848, Alemany served for two years as the Provincial of the American Dominicans.

In the summer of 1850, Pope Pius IX summoned the Dominican friar to Rome and on June 30, 1850, the 36-year-old Alemany was consecrated "Bishop of Monterey, Upper California." On September 9, 1850, California became the 31st state. One month later, accompanied by Dominican friar Francis Sadoc Vilarrasa and Dominican sister Mary Goemaere of Belgium, Monterey's new bishop set sail out of New York on a vessel bound for San Francisco. (San Francisco was for the first three years, part of the newly formed Monterey Diocese.)

Shortly after his arrival in San Francisco, Alemany said his first mass at the small wooden church of St. Francis of Assisi on Sunday, December 8, 1850. On that day he presented his sermons in English, Spanish and French. He left San Francisco on December 14 and headed south to minister to all the members of his Monterey Diocese. The Archbishop would return to San Francisco as a "full-time resident" on July 29, 1853. This newly formed Archdiocese had an estimated Catholic population of 40,000.

While Alemany's accomplishments in San Francisco are too many to list, they include the construction of Old St. Mary's Church (still standing but then called St. Mary's Cathedral), at the corner of California Street and Grant Avenue. He also built an extensive system of schools, hospitals, churches, and charity institutions, as well as homes for the aged. In 1854, at the invitation of the Archbishop, Sister Mary Baptist Russell of the Sisters of Mercy led a party of eight sisters from Ireland, all the way to the wilds of San Francisco to minister to the health, educational and spiritual needs of the citizens of this Bay City boomtown. Many religious orders dedicated to the ministry of education and/or health, answered Alemany's call to provide for San Francisco. These orders included the Jesuits, Franciscans, Christian Brothers, Daughters of Charity, Presentation Sisters, Sisters of Notre Dame de Namur and many, many more fellow Dominicans.

In August of 1860, Archbishop Alemany purchased land on the slopes of Lone Mountain for the Calvary Catholic Cemetery. Calvary was 49.2 acres of land bounded by Geary, Turk, St. Joseph and Masonic Streets. There was a chapel built at its entrance and once a month, the Archbishop rode on horseback from Old St. Mary's to say Mass.

In November of 1883, Archbishop Alemany traveled 1,000 miles to Ogden, Utah to welcome his coadjutor and successor, the Most Reverend Patrick William Riordan, and on December 28, 1884, Archbishop Alemany resigned his New World diocese and retired to Catalonia. He died in Valencia on April 14, 1888 and was buried in the Church of Sant Domènec in Vic. In 1965, his body was brought back to San Francisco and buried here at Holy Cross. (The sepulcher of Archbishop Alemany is located in the central apse of the Holy Cross Mausoleum, an area reserved for the burial of archbishops of San Francisco.)

THE PURCHASE OF HOLY CROSS CATHOLIC CEMETERY – COLMA

First established as grazing land for Mission Dolores and the Presidio of San Francisco, Rancho Buri Buri once covered approximately 15,000 acres. It stretched across parts of (what is now) Colma, South San Francisco, San Bruno, Millbrae and Burlingame. In 1827, Mexican Governor José María de Echeandía granted permission for Presidio-stationed Sub lieutenant José Antonio Sánchez to occupy the ranch for grazing and agricultural purposes. In 1835, the Mexican land grant was given to Sánchez by Alta California Governor José Castro. At the death of Sánchez in 1843, the ranch lands were divided among his ten children.

Over time the land would be sold off, in portions, to folks like Darius Ogden Mills, who named his estate Millbrae, and Charles Lux – whose purchase would lead to the establishment of South San Francisco.

All the while the population of San Francisco grew. But of course the City, at a size of 46.7 square miles, did not.

When Archbishop Riordan's predecessor arrived in San Francisco in 1850, the U.S. Census listed the population at 21,000. By 1880, the population was just shy of 234,000. And in the early 1880s, property owners living near the "big four" cemeteries in San Francisco – Laurel Hill, Calvary, the Masonic Cemetery and the Independent Order of Odd Fellows Cemetery (all in the Lone Mountain-Laurel Heights area) – began to make noise about the removal of those cemeteries. How could they build up the neighborhood if so much of it was taken up by folks no longer contributing to the City's welfare! Many San Franciscans joined in this fight. While their wishes would take a number of decades, litigation, and multiple elections to come to fruition, the new Archbishop fully realized that Calvary Cemetery was reaching its capacity.

In 1886, Archbishop Patrick Riordan purchased 300 acres of Rancho Buri Buri farmland, land rich in potato and cabbage crops, to build a new Catholic cemetery just five miles south of San Francisco in a town that would eventually be known as Colma. There were a lot of naysayers. People claimed that no one would want to travel that far to bury their dead. But in the early days of June 1887, Holy Cross opened its gates and two funeral carriages raced from San Francisco, so that the deceased they bore could be the first buried at this new cemetery. On June 7, 1887, Timothy Buckley's coachman won that race though admittedly, the late Bridget Martin has the more accessible real estate located within an easy walking distance from the cemetery's entrance gates. (Mr. Buckley's vault is in Section J. Mrs. Martin's monument is in Section E.)

Indeed, Archbishop Riordan had tremendous foresight. Horse-drawn carriages could head south on Mission Street to this new cemetery town. Southern Pacific railroad had assumed ownership of the San Francisco and San Jose railroad and Colma was a stop. By 1891, the San Francisco and San Mateo Railway brought in the electric streetcar line and San Mateo County granted franchises for the railway to build from the county line to Holy Cross Cemetery.

Holy Cross is the first and the largest of a total of 17 cemeteries built in a town which currently claims one million and a half interred and a living population of seventeen hundred. Significant portions of the acres the Archbishop purchased are still to be developed, and as Holy Cross celebrates its 125th anniversary, it already looks forward to the next 125 years of serving the needs of the Catholic community.

ARCHBISHOPS OF SAN FRANCISCO
1853 THROUGH 2012

Joseph Sadoc Alemany
(1853-1884)

Patrick William Riordan
(1884-1914)

Edward Joseph Hanna
(1915-1935)

John Joseph Mitty
(1938-1961)

Joseph Thomas McGucken
(1962-1977)

John Raphael Quinn
(1977-1995)

William Joseph Levada
(1995-2005)

George Hugh Niederauer
(2006-2012)

Salvatore Joseph Cordileone
(Installation Mass
October 4, 2012)

WHO'S BURIED IN HOLY CROSS?

Like all cemeteries, Holy Cross contains story after story, 370,000 stories in this case, of those who gave us a history from which to build. But many of these stories cannot be found in written records. People often grieve in solitude and the stories of those they have loved are left only within private heartaches. There was also the real and vital loss of records, following the great San Francisco earthquake of 1906. On April 18, at 5:12 a.m., an earthquake with a magnitude of 7.8 on the Richter scale, lasting 45 to 60 seconds, struck San Francisco. It ruptured the ground surface along the San Andreas Fault for about 290 miles and was felt from southern Oregon to south of Los Angeles and inland as far as central Nevada. Included in its path of destruction were city records, including birth certificates, completely destroyed in the earthquake and subsequent fire.

In the 1908 Lawson report – a study of the 1906 quake managed and edited by Professor Andrew Lawson of the University of California – it was reported that in Colma, "over 75% of the monuments in Holy Cross were thrown down or twisted on their base." It also noted damage to the Holy Cross train station.

So it can be said that both privacy and natural disaster have left the pages of many men, women and children who have gone before us – pages still yet to be filled. In addition, as we reach back not so far into history, women and their deeds were often a quiet reference, if indeed referenced at all.

With all this in mind, as Holy Cross recognizes its 125th year with a book which celebrates each and every life that has been laid to rest within our gates, we can only hint of a few of the "famous" we know. All the stories herein are snippets, not meant to explain the full measure of a man or a woman or a child, but to hint of the life which passed. For some, we have relied on old accounts, where the accuracy of the detail might be lost to the substance of the individual. We look towards descendants and scholars to help us right any errors. But then, this is only volume one…

Winifred Sweet Black Bonfils
Public Domain Photo

FAMOUS
WOMEN

BONFILS, WINIFRED SWEET BLACK (1863-1936). Bonfils was the fourth of five children born in Chilton, Wisconsin to attorney Benjamin Jeffrey Sweet, a Union officer in the Civil War, and Lovisa Loveland (Denslow) Sweet. Her father died when she was 11 and her mother when she was 15. She lived with her older sister Adele in Chicago until she headed out West in 1890. She was hired by William Randolph Hearst as a reporter for the San Francisco Examiner. As was customary for female reporters at the time, she took on a pseudonym "Annie Laurie." She covered many stories for Hearst including the 1900 Galveston Hurricane, the 1906 earthquake, and reported from Europe during the First World War. Her first husband was Orlow Black. Her second husband was Charles Bonfils. She was considered a top-of-the-line journalist and a colorful personality. She wrote her last story at age 72 and died at 73. By order of Mayor Angelo J. Rossi, Winifred's body lay in state in the rotunda of San Francisco's City Hall and special civic exercises were conducted in her honor. *(K-14-8-3-7)*

CARLSON, CONSTANCE BROWN (1912-2011). A lifelong San Francisco resident, Carlson attended UC Berkeley and received her teaching credential from San Francisco State College. As such she served for many years as a substitute teacher at San Francisco's West Portal and Commodore Sloat schools. She was the granddaughter of California pioneers, the sister of Edmund G. "Pat" Brown, who served as California's governor twice, and the aunt of Jerry Brown, who to date has served three terms as California's governor. *(K-7-10-4-11)*

DAVIES, LOUISE M. (1900-1998). She grew up on her grandfather's farm in Plumas County, near the town of Quincy. After she graduated from a convent school in Rio Vista, she worked as a stenographer in Oakland for $25 a week. Early in childhood she got it in her head that she would either be an actress or a nun, so she headed to Los Angeles to give acting a try. She met Ralph K. Davies in July of 1924, on a vacation to the Russian River. They married in 1925. Her husband, at one point the VP of Standard Oil, went out on his own and amassed a fortune from buying oil concessions all over the world. Louise, who never forgot her roots, donated $5 million to the construction of the San Francisco Symphony's permanent concert hall, which opened in 1980 as Davies Symphony Hall. She later donated another $3 million to provide an endowment to attract guest conductors. She also gave millions to other San Francisco charities. *(H-20-76)*

FOLEY, WILMA SIMPSON (1903-1995). She was born in North Liberty, Iowa, and lived there until she was 18 years old. She studied at UC Berkeley where she earned a Master's degree in chemistry and graduated cum laude. She was the first woman professor in science to teach at UC Berkeley. She paid for her own education by baking fancy cakes for the wealthy women in Piedmont. She married John F. Foley in 1929 and went on to open a successful dress shop. *(St. Rose of Lima-16-49)*

FOLGER, ABIGAIL (1943-1969). Born in San Francisco, she was the great-granddaughter of J.A. Folger, the founder of Folger Coffee Company. Her parents were Inez Mejia, the daughter of a consul general of El Salvador and Peter Folger, the long-time Chairman of the Board and President of Folger. Abigail graduated with honors from Radcliffe in 1964, where she was a member of the college's musical theatre group, The Gilbert and Sullivan Players. Following Radcliffe, Abigail received her graduate degree in Art History from Harvard. She worked at a number of art galleries and bookstores in New York, and in 1968 returned to California with Polish actor and writer Voytek Frykowski. The couple moved to Los Angeles and became friends with a number of celebrity neighbors who included French-Polish film director Roman Polanski and his wife, actress Sharon Tate. During this time, Abigail became a volunteer social worker, donating her time to the Los Angeles County Welfare Department and to the Haight-Ashbury Medical Clinic in San Francisco. With so many plans for the future in front of her, on August 9, 1969, Abigail was one of seven adults, including actress Sharon Tate, who was eight months pregnant, brutally murdered by Charles Manson. *(Mausoleum-N-205)*

FORBES, KATHRYN (1908-1966). "Kathryn Forbes" was the pen name of Kathryn Anderson McClean. Born in San Francisco, Kathryn Anderson was the granddaughter of Norwegian immigrants. Her first writing jobs were as a radio scriptwriter. She then began writing short stories. In 1943, she published "Mama's Bank Account," which inspired the hugely popular John Van Druten play "I Remember Mama." The play was subsequently turned into a movie starring Irene Dunne as Mama and Barbara Bel Geddes as Mama's aspiring writer daughter. The story was also turned into a CBS television series, "Mama," which ran from 1949 to 1957. Twice her novel made it to the stage as a musical. In 1947, Forbes published another novel, "Transfer Point." *(5-8-35)*

HOFFMAN, CLAIRE GIANNINI (1904-1997). The daughter of A.P. Giannini, the founder of Bank of America, Hoffman attended Mills College in Oakland, and became her father's traveling companion and confidante on many of his business trips nationwide and abroad. In 1930, she married Clifford "Biff" Hoffman, an investment banker and former All-American track and football star at Stanford. (He died in 1954.) In 1949, she was appointed to her father's seat on Bank of America's board, becoming the bank's first woman director. In 1952, she became a member of the bank's General Executive Committee. In the 1950s, the Eisenhower Administration chose Mrs. Hoffman to serve on the National Council of Consultants to the U.S. Small Business Administration. She would serve as a member on many more international and national economic and banking committees. Additionally, she was appointed to numerous panels and commissions by President Lyndon Johnson and President Richard Nixon. She was widely honored for her achievements and contributions including, in 1975, by the California State Legislature, for her outstanding record of dedication and service. Prior to her death, she established The Claire Giannini Fund in honor of the unwavering principles of her father to, "regularly contribute to causes that place the needs of ordinary people above private ambition, prioritizing the welfare of children, and the importance of education for all." *(Mausoleum-1-318)*

MARTIN, BRIDGET (Died June 5, 1887, age 84). A native of the Parish of Kilcornan, County Galway, Ireland, she was married to Thomas and resided at 1827-1/2 Bush Street, San Francisco. Mrs. Martin was the first woman to be buried at Holy Cross and the second person. Her funeral carriage, which took off from St. John's Church in San Francisco, arrived just a horse's length behind that of the Cemetery's first interred, Timothy Buckley. (Or so the rumor goes.) Her monument was erected by her beloved sons. (The cost of her plot was $153.60.) *(E-5-1-1)*

MEIÈRE, HILDRETH (1892-1961). Born in New York, Meière was an art deco muralist and mosaicist, painter and decorative artist and was recognized as being the most distinguished and prolific in her field. Included among her works are the three roundels – "Song," "Drama" and "Dance" that she designed for the 50th Street facade of Radio City Music Hall. Along with Radio City Music Hall, Meière installed works at hundreds of public and religious buildings including Temple Emanu-El in Manhattan, the National Academy of Science in Washington, D.C. and the Cathedral Basilica of St. Louis. She was honored in

1928 by the Architectural League of New York with a Gold Medal in Mural Decoration for her work on the Nebraska State Capitol. In 1956 she was awarded a Fine Arts Medal by the American Institute of Architects. This was the first time that either medal was given to a woman. *(1-20-21-9)*

NOLAN, MAE (1886-1973). Born in San Francisco, Nolan attended St. Vincent's Convent and Ayres Business College. She was the fourth woman to serve in Congress and the first woman elected to serve from California. Elected by special election on January 23, 1923, to fill the vacancy caused by the death of her husband, John Ignatius Nolan, Mae served as a Republican to the Sixty-seventh and the Sixty-eighth Congresses. She was the first woman to be elected to her husband's Congressional seat. *(1-38-6-3)*

OTTO, MARIE KENDRICK (1908-2003). The third generation San Franciscan and the daughter of industrialist and civic leader Charles Kendrick, who helped create the War Memorial complex, Otto graduated from Berkeley in 1928. She was a 32-year member of the San Francisco Symphony Board of Governors from which, she never missed a meeting. She was a longtime member of the symphony executive committee and active in the fundraising campaign that led to the construction of Davies Hall, which opened in 1980. She was one of the founders and primary endowers of the innovative Adventures in Music program, in which symphony musicians perform at public schools and students attend symphony youth concerts at Davies Hall. *(Mausoleum-4-PS1-5th)*

QUARTARARO, FLORENCE (1922-1994). A graduate of San Francisco State College, the San Francisco-born Italian American soprano made her operatic stage debut in 1946, at the Metropolitan Opera Company (New York). She sang the role of Micaela in "Carmen." The next season at the Met she sang in "Otello" and she appeared regularly at the Met, singing nine leading roles. In 1947, she made her San Francisco debut as Donna Elvira in Mozart's "Don Giovanni." For a decade she performed with both the Metropolitan and the San Francisco opera companies. In 1957 she brought her career to a halt to devote time to her marriage to Italian basso Italo Tajo and their family. *(Our Lady of Peace-F-N338)*

Maude Fay Symington

SYMINGTON, MAUDE FAY (1878-1964). Born in San Francisco, the world-renowned American soprano studied in Dresden, Germany. She made her debut in 1906 as Marguerite in "Faust" at the Munich Royal Opera. At the outbreak of the First World War she remained in Germany and did Red Cross work. In 1916, she returned to the States for her Metropolitan Opera debut as Sieglinde in "Die Walküre." She was particularly distinguished in Wagnerian roles. She met Powers Symington, who had graduated from the U.S. Naval Academy in 1892, in San Francisco in 1922. They married six months later in the private chapel of San Francisco Archbishop Edward J Hanna. Maude's younger brother was Paul Burgess Fay, and Paul was the father of Sarah Fay (Tobin) and Paul "Red" Burgess Fay Jr. Paul Jr. was a close friend and shipmate of President John F. Kennedy. More on Maude Fay Symington can be found in her book, "Living in Awe," a compilation of her memoirs. *(D-4-9-2)*

TERRANOVA, JOSEPHINE (1889-1981). Born in Sicily, Terranova arrived in New York when she was 8, and went to live with her aunt and uncle. In 1906, Terranova stabbed and killed her aunt and uncle, Concetta and Gaetano Riggio, with a butcher knife. In court she offered a harrowing account of the continual sexual and physical abuse they subjected her to. She was charged with murder in the first degree and a guilty verdict would have meant death by electric chair. Medical experts for the defense testified Josephine was insane. The trial was a sensation and led to widespread public debate on psychiatric expertise in the courtroom. Her lawyer, John Palmieri, was successful with his client's insanity plea and Josephine went free. Allegedly with the financial assistance of William Randolph Hearst, Terranova and her husband Giuseppe (she was married at 17), moved to San Francisco where they lived quietly and raised their five children. Her great granddaughter, who lives in the Bay Area, and who knew her great grandmother, didn't know anything about the circumstances that befell Josephine in New York. In fact none of Josephine's children, or grandchildren or great grandchildren knew about it until after Josephine's death when they all found out about it together. "For me, my grandmother was a wonderful woman who taught me how to cook Italian food," her great granddaughter said. "She would tell stories of her youth, and her years living in San Francisco with my great grandfather, and about raising her children." *(5-10-99)*

THIERIOT, KATHLEEN de YOUNG (1889-1954). The third daughter of Chronicle founder Michael de Young, the San Francisco native married the New Jersey born Ferdinand Thieriot, an investor, on January 28, 1914. Kathleen's husband was the cousin of Eugene de Sabla, Jr. a cofounder of Pacific Gas & Electric. The couple had two sons, Michael de Young and Ferdinand "Peter." Son Michael was the San Francisco Chronicle publisher from 1955-1977. Son Peter was the Chronicle's circulation manager. On July 26, 1956, 35-year-old Peter and his wife Frances died when the ocean liner they were traveling on, the SS Andrea Doria, collided with the passenger ship MS Stockholm and sank. Mrs. Thieriot is the great grandmother of the 1988-born American actor Max Thieriot. *(I-21-16-UGV)*

TOBIN, AGNES (1864-1939). Irish author William Butler Yeats called her, "the greatest poet that America has produced since Walt Whitman." The daughter of Richard Tobin, co-founder of Hibernia S&L, Agnes was known more as a translator in her lifetime. Among other lauded works, she translated two of the tragedians of classical Athens, Euripides and Sophocles, into English. She also translated Jean Racine's five-act dramatic tragedy "Phè-dre," written in Alexandrine verse, into English – a project which took two and 1/2 years. Her literary friends included Joseph Conrad, Alice Meynell, Sir Edmund Gosse, Arthur Symons, Francis Thompson and Joaquin Miller. *(D-11-9-3-12)*

TOBIN, SARAH FAY "SALLY" (1925-1996). The daughter of construction magnate Paul Burgess Fay Sr., president of Fay Improvement Co., which built roads and sewers throughout San Francisco, Sally was born in San Francisco and raised in Woodside. Sally's marriage in 1952 to Michael Henry de Young Tobin, a grandson of Chronicle founder Michael H. de Young, was a San Francisco social event. She was also the sister of Paul "Red" Burgess Fay Jr., who met John F. Kennedy when they were both in the Navy, and who joined his administration as Undersecretary of the Navy and then wrote a best-selling book about their friendship. (Sally's aunt was American soprano Maude Fay Symington.) Before Sally's marriage to Tobin, she was president of The Spinsters of San Francisco, a community oriented social and philanthropic organization which was formed in 1929 as a sister organization to The Bachelors of San Francisco. Mrs. Tobin was a trustee of the Graduate Theological Union in Berkeley and active in such organizes as St. Elizabeth's Home and the Achievement Rewards for College Students Foundations. *(D-11-9-2-10)*

Jean Bartlett photo

FAMOUS MEN

Jean Bartlett photo

Joe DiMaggio Mausoleum

ALIOTO, JOSEPH (1916-1998). Joseph Alioto is memorialized at the Alioto/Veronese Plot at Holy Cross. Born in San Francisco, the son of a Sicilian immigrant, Alioto grew up in North Beach and attended Saints Peter and Paul Elementary School and Saint Ignatius College Preparatory. He was a magna cum laude graduate of St. Mary's College (California) and entered the law school at The Catholic University of America on a scholarship. He received his J.D. in 1940. He worked for the Justice Department's antitrust division and then for a wartime agency. He returned to San Francisco in 1946 and started his own law firm. When he entered the 1967 race for mayor of San Francisco, he was a little known candidate; but he took to the campaign trail with all the enthusiasm he held for the city he loved. He served as San Francisco Mayor from 1968 to 1976. A philanthropist and patron of the arts, Alioto is recognized for his efforts in bringing about the development of three signature projects – the Bay Area Rapid Transit System (BART), the Transamerica Pyramid and the Embarcadero Center. *(D-10-1-1-10)*

ATHERTON, FAXON D. (1815-1877). Born and educated in Massachusetts, Atherton went into the shipping and merchant business in his teens. He headed out to the Pacific coast in 1834 to work for a ship chandlery firm in Valparaiso, Chile. In 1836, Atherton came to California and worked as a clerk for Alpheus B. Thompson, an early California merchant engaged in the hides and tallow trade. Atherton became good friends with Thomas O. Larkin (who would become one of the original signers of the California constitution), and he and Larkin joined forces on several real estate and commercial ventures. In 1840, Atherton settled in Valparaiso and became a successful merchant dealing in hides and tallow, foodstuffs, and other commodities. He met his wife Dominga de Goñi in Chile and they married in 1843. The couple had seven children. Their son George married Gertrude Franklin Horn – one of California's most important authors. With the arrival of California's Gold Rush, Faxon Atherton amassed a fortune with his import/export shipping business. In 1860, Atherton liquidated his assets in Chile and reinvested his money in California. He also bought, at $10 an acre, 640 acres of land along the San Francisco-San Jose Railroad line known then as Fair Oaks where he built his home, "Valparaiso Park," several years later. On September 12, 1923, Fair Oaks was incorporated as the town of Atherton, in honor of the man who was one of the Southern Peninsula's first property owners. *(Mausoleum-D-PS-19-4th)*

BROWN, SR., EDMUND G. "PAT" (1905-1996). San Francisco born, Edmund Brown got his nickname "Pat" in seventh grade when he delivered a powerful speech to sell liberty bonds and ended it with the Patrick Henry quote, "Give me Liberty, or give me Death!" Thereinafter his classmates called him Patrick Henry Brown, eventually shortened to "Pat." Brown graduated from Lowell High School where he ran for 11 student offices and won each time. He received a law degree from the San Francisco Law School in 1927. He began his political career as a Republican, running for a seat in the State Assembly in 1928, a campaign which he lost. Four years later he became a Democrat. He ran unsuccessfully in 1939 for District Attorney of San Francisco, but won that seat in a 1943 election. He held that post until 1950, when he became California's Attorney General. In 1958, he was elected Governor of California and served two terms. In 1959, the California Governor signed the Fair Employment Practices Act (FEPA) that prohibits race discrimination in employment and public accommodations. His son Jerry Brown, to date, has served three terms as California's governor. *(D-10-1-4-8)*

BUCKLEY, TIMOTHY (Died June 5, 1887, age 46). Born in Ireland, Buckley was married and resided at 438 Minna Street, San Francisco. He was buried from St. Patrick's Church on June 7 and is noted as the first to be interred at Holy Cross with, rumor has it, his funeral carriage just edging out the funeral carriage of Mrs. Bridget Martin for that distinction. (The cost of his plot was $60.00.) *(J-1-2-4-10)*

BUFANO, BENNY (1898-1970). Italian-born, world-famous sculptor Bufano moved with his parents and 11 siblings to New York when he was three. He spent his childhood in New

York City and studied under private tutors and attended the Arts Student League of New York. In 1915, his work was signaled out at a prestigious Whitney Museum of American Art contest by the New York Times and by President Theodore Roosevelt and his career took off. Bufano came to San Francisco in 1915 to work on a sculpture for the 1915 Panama-Pacific International Exposition. He would live and work in San Francisco for most of his life. An avowed peace activist, legend had it that Bufano chopped off his trigger finger and mailed it to President Woodrow Wilson to protest World War I. (His wife reported, however, that he accidentally lost two joints of his right index finger to an electric saw.) Friends included Mahatma Gandhi and a number of his sculptures are dedicated to peace. Many of his works are found throughout the Bay Area. At Holy Cross, he is interred in front of one of his creations, "Saint Francis, the Prince of Peace," in Section W. *(W-1F-35/36)*

CARCIONE, JOE "GREEN GROCER" (1914-1988). In 1933, when Carcione was 19, he started working in his father's wholesale market and a career was born. He eventually operated his own produce import/export business in South San Francisco at the Golden Gate Produce Terminal II. In the '70s, he got a daily spot on local news radio station KCBS to promote his enthusiasm for fruits and vegetables. His catch-phrase was "but I wanna tell ya folks." His television show, "The Green Grocer," was picked up nationwide in syndication, playing five days a week and his listeners were always entertained by his pronunciation of vegetables ("veja-tobbles"). The Green Grocer also had a column in the San Francisco Chronicle. He was married to Madeline (Ahern) and they had three children. His son Peter is the president of the employee-owned Carcione Fresh Produce Company in San Francisco. *(All Saints Mausoleum-ANT-205)*

COOPER, JUAN BAUTISTA ROGERS "DON JUAN EL MANCO" (ONE-ARMED JOHN) (1791-1872). Born John Rogers Cooper (he changed his name during the time he was a Mexican citizen), Cooper was the son of Captain Thomas Cooper and Anne Rogers. It is guessed that he was born in England but what is known is that as an infant, he was baptized on the English Channel Island of Alderney. When Cooper was quite young, his father was lost at sea. He and his mother headed to Massachusetts. (Note his mother remarried and Cooper's half-brother was Thomas O. Larkin, an instrumental force behind California's admittance to the Union.) Somewhere in Cooper's youth, the nerves in his left arm were injured in a knife fight, which gave him his nickname "One-Armed John." In his lifetime, Cooper had great success with many jobs and/or titles – shipmaster, merchant, adventurer, trader, ranchero, Monterey Harbormaster, landowner. He served on a number of ships, and when he arrived in San Francisco in 1823, he arrived as Master of the ship Rover. In 1827, Cooper married the older sister of General Mariano Vallejo (for whom the Northern California town is named), and throughout his many engaging days, this pre-gold rush California pioneer knew and worked with the prominent people of his time. In his life Cooper would be a British citizen, American citizen, Mexican citizen and then again an American citizen. The latter took place in 1848 by virtue of the treaty of Guadalupe Hidalgo. Cooper died in his San Francisco home in February of 1872. He was the grandfather of Andrew Molera. *(I-4-2-4)*

CUNEO, JOSEPH (1834-1902). Born in Genoa, Italy, Cuneo was raised on a farm. When he was 14, he sailed to New York and got his first job making figures in wax at $3.50 a month plus board. He also did picture framing, worked at a candy store, and ran his own market. At age 19, he decided to see what the California Gold Rush was all about and arrived in San Francisco with $75 in his pocket. His own prospecting days were not rewarding, but once he began investing in various business ventures, his finances improved. In the gold country, he started a store and saloon which were both successful. In 1863 he married his wife Mary, and as the years progressed the couple had 14 children. In 1870, he opened a store on Taylor Street in San Francisco. At the same time he began purchasing real estate and also continued managing his mining interests. He amassed a great fortune in real estate. In 1892, his daughter Clorinda married A.P. Giannini, the founder of Bank of America. *(D-13-1-1/ 4-OGV)*

DAVIES, RALPH K. (1897-1971). Davies began his career with Standard Oil. He met the love of his life, Louise M. Stivers, when he was in the early stages of becoming a self-made millionaire. He proposed to Louise on the shore of Lake Merritt in Oakland and they married in 1925. By that time, Davies had already set his sights on being Standard Oil's president and by the beginning of the Second World War, he was vice president. During the War, he served as Deputy Petroleum Administrator for Secretary of the Interior Harold Ickes. Following the War, he returned to Standard Oil. But after he was bypassed for the presidency, he set out on his own. He made millions buying oil concessions all over the world. He eventually ran American President Lines and the Natomas Company. An extremely generous benefactor to many, many charitable organizations, he additionally sat on the board of San Francisco's Franklin Hospital. Following his death, the hospital was renamed the Ralph K. Davies Medical Center. It is now the Davies Campus of the California Pacifica Medical Center. *(H-19-76)*

De LATOUR, GEORGES (1856-1940). Born in Bordeaux, France, de Latour attended the Jesuit College where he studied to be a chemist. When he was 26 he sailed to New York. Not long after he headed west to California. He did a bit of mining, then worked as a chemist in San Francisco from 1884 to 1888. He next went to work in San Jose and became a successful manufacturer of cream of tartar. In 1895, he returned to San Francisco and constructed a refinery. He sold that, bought four acres of vines in Rutherford, which he named Beaulieu "beautiful place," and in 1899 he founded Beaulieu Vineyard. Anticipating the onset of Prohibition, he made his fortune stockpiling sweet wine which he sold at a high markup right before Prohibition began on January 16, 1920. His relationship with the Catholic Church allowed him to make sacramental wine through and beyond Prohibition's end in 1933. In 1937, he headed to France in search of a winemaker. He returned to Rutherford with the legendary enologist André Tchelistcheff. *(I-21-19-OGV)*

De YOUNG, MICHAEL HENRY (1849-1925). Born in St. Louis, Missouri, Michael moved to San Francisco with his older brother Charles, their widowed mother Amelia and youngest brother Gustavus, when he was a young teen. There he and Charles reinvented the family, which was of Dutch Jewish descent, as descendants of French aristocracy. As teens, using a $20 gold piece borrowed from the landlord, Michael and Charles founded The Daily Dramatic Chronicle, the precursor to the San Francisco Chronicle. Originally a small daily theatrical 4-page advertising sheet, the Daily Dramatic had its first issue on January 16, 1865. Three months later Abraham Lincoln was assassinated (April 14, 1865). His death appeared in their first "extra" edition which beat out all the other daily journals by several hours. This legitimized their newspaper and with the brothers' noted ability to "scratch their way to the top," they did rise to the top. In 1868, the paper became The Daily Morning Chronicle. The brothers' credo was "entertain and incite the population." Their newspaper thrived. In 1880, Charles de Young was murdered by Isaac Milton Kalloch, the son of San Francisco Mayor Isaac Smith Kalloch, and Michael took over the paper. In 1884, Michael was shot by Adolph Spreckels, which he survived and for which Spreckels was acquitted on a "claim of reasonable cause." Michael converted to Catholicism after marrying his wife, Katherine I. Deane. They had four daughters, including Kathleen de Young Thieriot. (Kathleen's son, Michael, was the San Francisco Chronicle publisher from 1955-1977.) Michael and Katherine also had a son, Charles, who died in 1913. San Francisco's famous de Young Museum, a fine arts museum in Golden Gate Park, is more formally called the M. H. de Young Memorial Museum, after its namesake. *(1-20-17-OGV)*

public domain photo

Michael de Young

DiMAGGIO, JOSEPH P. (1914-1999). The son of a fisherman, DiMaggio was born in Martinez, California and moved with his family to the North Beach neighborhood of San Francisco when he was one. Joe and his brothers Vince and Dominic used to practice baseball in various vacant sandlots in the neighborhood, especially one known as "The Horses' Lot," where they'd occasionally hit a passing streetcar with a sailing ball. In 1933, DiMaggio was signed on full-time to the roster of the San Francisco Seals, the City's Pacific Coast League team. On May 3, 1936, DiMaggio made his debut in the Major Leagues as a New York Yankee, where he stayed until after the 1951 season (he spent 1943-45 in the U.S. Army). Known as "Joltin' Joe" and the "Yankee Clipper," the center fielder was a three-time MVP winner and 13-time All-Star. He had a 56-game hitting streak in 1941, a record that still stands as one of the greatest achievements in baseball history. His first marriage to Dorothy Arnold lasted from 1939-1944 and produced a son, Joe DiMaggio Jr., who died in 1999, five months after his dad. Joe's second marriage in 1954 to Marilyn Monroe lasted less than a year but they remained friends until her death in 1962. *(I-11-6/7-OGV)*

DINAN, JEREMIAH F. (1862-1950). Born in Ireland, Dinan immigrated to San Francisco were he joined the Police Department in 1888. In 1898 he was promoted to Detective Sergeant. In 1905, he was named SFPD Chief. On the evening of April 17, 1906, the Chief attended Enrico Caruso's performance in Bizet's "Carmen" at the Grand Opera House at Third and Mission streets. The next morning at 5:12 a.m., the San Francisco earthquake struck. The Police Department had no plans for such a catastrophe and communication with outlying stations was severed. Within two hours, Dinan established a makeshift disaster headquarters in the basement of the half-ruined Hall of Justice, maintaining it until 4:30 p.m. when it became apparent the Hall would be destroyed by fire. He additionally saw to the removal of the Hall's records (what Hall records he could save), sending them over to Portsmouth Square, where cinders constantly threatened the canvas that covered them – resolved by police officers pouring bottles of beer on the canvas, retrieved from the saloon across the street. A few months down the road still in 1906, San Francisco became embroiled in political fallout as public officials, including Mayor Eugene Schmitz, were taken into court on multiple charges of graft and corruption. In 1907, Dinan, facing a charge of perjury in regards to his testimony at Mayor Schmitz's trial, resigned as Chief. He did not, however, resign as a police detective. He was eventually cleared of the criminal charge of perjury and restored to duty as a detective. When he retired from the SFPD, he had served for forty-three years, eight months and fifteen days. *(I-1-2-2)*

DONNELLY, JOHN T. (1885-1904). On April 13, 1904, the USS Missouri was engaged in target practice when a twelve-inch gun in the after turret, flared back hot gasses into the turret when the breach was opened for reloading. This set a bag of propellant on fire which spread into the ammunition handling chamber below. Thirty-six of the ship's officers and crew perished and one was 19-year-old John Donnelly. Born in Chicago and raised in California, Donnelly was one of three men, all gunners' mates, awarded a Medal of Honor for prompt actions which brought the fire under control and saved many lives and prevented the loss of the warship. The enlisted men of the Battleship Missouri built a monument to their departed comrade at Holy Cross. "He displayed a heroism and a devotion to duty," their inscription reads, "which won the unstinted praise, not alone of his captain and officers, but of the President of the United States and the Secretary of the Navy." *(D-8-4-3)*

DOUGLASS, LEON F. (1869-1940). An American inventor and a Vice President of the Victor Talking Machine Company – where he created the advertising campaign of a terrier listening to "His Master's Voice" – Douglass registered about fifty patents, mostly for film and sound recording. Born in Nebraska, 9-year-old Douglass had to support his family when his dad went blind. He apprenticed to a printer. He then became one of the first telephone operators in Lincoln. By 16, he was managing his work place, and at 18, he became district manager. He started registering patents, beginning with a phonograph coin slot. He often sold patents, making $500 here, $2,000 there and more, which would send him on his next quest. (Inventions would include the zoom lens and the first patented process for natural color motion pictures.) In 1896, he headed out to San Francisco and met with Peter Bacigalupi, the San Francisco distributor of Thomas Edison's inventions. He also met Peter's stepdaughter Victoria Adams. The two married and moved to Chicago. Working with Talking Machine Co. of Chicago, and making about $5,000 a year, at age 31, Douglass resigned and went to work for Eldridge Johnson (Victor Talking Machine). Just a few years later, Victor was spending $4 million per year on advertising. In 1906, worn out from too much work, Douglass had a nervous breakdown and spent two years in San Rafael recuperating. Extremely wealthy because of his stockholding, Douglass continued to invent from his home. In 1921, he purchased a 52-room mansion in Menlo Park, built a sound and motion picture workshop and additionally built a swimming pool so he could experiment with underwater photography. *(D-12-13-1/4-OGV)*

DOWNEY, JOHN G. (1827-1894). Born in Roscommon County, Ireland, Downey was the seventh Governor of California (1860-1862), and the first Governor to be foreign-born. He arrived in the States at age fifteen. At 19, he co-owned a pharmacy in Cincinnati. In 1949, gold brought him to Grass Valley, California. After a short try at mining, he headed to San Francisco where he worked as a pharmacist with Henry Johnson & Company. In December of 1850, he and Dr. James P. McFarland opened a drug store in the Los Angeles area which was very successful, bringing Downey a net worth of $30,000 in just three years. Downey became a U.S. citizen in 1851. He served for a year in the lower house California State Assembly and was

public domain photo
John G. Downey

elected Lieutenant Governor in 1859. Five days after being sworn in, Downey succeeded Governor Milton Latham who resigned in order to fill the vacancy left by the death of State Senator David C. Broderick, who was killed in a duel in Daly City. Downey's veto of the "bulkhead" bill, which would have allowed ownership of San Francisco's waterfront by a monopoly, made Downey a hero to San Franciscans. When he arrived in San Francisco shortly after his veto, the "entire population was at the ferry to salute him," and they carried him "in triumph through the streets of the City." Downey, California is named after him. He was originally interred at Old Calvary Cemetery in Los Angeles. When the cemetery relocated, Downey was moved to Holy Cross. *(E-1-1/2-1/4)*

FAIR, JAMES G. (1831-1894). Born near Belfast, County Tyrone, Ireland, Fair immigrated to the States in 1843. The family settled in Illinois. Following the 1849 Gold Rush, Fair, who had studied business, ventured off to California. He engaged in gold mining where he earned a reputation for understanding ore bodies and was employed as superintendent of various mines. He headed off to Virginia City, Nevada in 1860. By then he had real estate interests in San Francisco. In 1867, he met fellow Irishman John William Mackay who hired him to run his Rising Star Mine. Working with investors (James Flood and William O'Brien), the four men took control of various mines and turned a profit. In 1873, while exploring the Consolidated Virginia and California Mine in Virginia City, Fair and Mackay discovered the "Big Bonanza," the greatest silver mine ever found, $100 million of silver. Fair would go on to serve as a Nevada Senator from March of 1881 to March of 1887. He would additionally amass great wealth from investments in railroads, property and buildings. After his death, his daughter Tessie Fair Oelrichs hired James and Merrit Reid to design a six-hundred room hotel in the Italian Renaissance style and named it The Fairmont. The San Francisco Fairmont still stands today. *(H-1-1-1/2-OGV)*

FLOURNOY, GEORGE M. (1832-1889). Born in Georgia, Confederate officer Flournoy graduated from law school at Tuskegee, Alabama in 1853. In 1854, he and his first wife Eugenia (Haralson) moved to Austin, Texas where he opened a law practice. After his wife's death, he married Virginia (Holman) in 1858. From 1860-1862 he served as Texas Attorney General. Flournoy, who coauthored the Texas Declaration of Causes for Secession in 1861, resigned as attorney general in January of 1862 to organize the Sixteenth Texas Infantry regiment of Walker's Texas Division. He served as the colonel of the regiment throughout the War. When the Confederate government fell, he fled to Mexico and served for a time with Maximilian's forces. He eventually returned to Texas and practiced law. In 1876, he moved to California and continued working in the legal field. His son George, Jr. would go on to serve as San Francisco City and County Attorney. *(Calvary-12-83-1/2)*

FOX, CHARLES F. "CHARLIE" (1921-2004). Born in the Bronx, Fox broke into Major League Baseball in September of 1942 with the New York Giants. From 1943-46 he served in the U.S. Navy. At the end of the Second World War, he returned to the Giants as a player-manager in their minor-league clubs. When the Giants relocated to San Francisco in 1958, he went with them. During his time in the minors, Fox helped develop, among others, first baseman Willie McCovey. Moving back into the majors in May of 1970, Fox led the Giants to a division title in 1971. Starting in 1976, Fox went on to work in various capacities, from general manager to scout, with the Montreal Expos, the Chicago Cubs and the New York Yankees. He finished out his career as a scout for the Houston Astros. *(All Saints Mausoleum-JAM-516E)*

GIANNINI, AMADEO PETER "A.P." (1870-1949). Born in San Jose, Giannini's parents, Luigi and Virginia, were immigrants from Genoa. His father, a farmer, died when A.P. was only seven in a fight over a dollar. His mother's second marriage was to grocer Lorenzo Scatena, and at age 14, Giannini quit school to assist him. The business thrived but at age 31, A.P. was tired of the grocery business and sold his half interest in the company to employees and retired. By invitation, Giannini joined the board of the Columbus Savings & Loan Society in San Francisco's North Beach. He wanted to lend money to the working class which the bank was strongly against. So, he raised $150,000 and opened the Bank of Italy. Through his loans and faith in "everyman," he is credited with jump starting the wine industry as well creating a motion-picture loan division which helped build United Artists. In the aftermath of the 1906 earthquake, he immediately set up a temporary bank and made loans and collected deposits, with all the people the other banks didn't want to work with – often on no more than a handshake. By the mid 1920s, he owned the third largest bank in the nation. In 1930, Bank of Italy became Bank of America. *(H-1-4-4-UGV)*

HEALY, CAPTAIN MICHAEL A.

(1839-1904). Michael Healey was born near Macon, Georgia. His father was an Irish plantation owner and his mother was a former slave. He began his career at sea at the age of 15 as a cabin boy aboard the American East Indian clipper Jumna. An expert seaman, he rose to the rank of officer on merchant vessels. In 1864, he applied and was accepted as a Third Lieutenant in the U.S. Revenue Marine. President Abraham Lincoln signed Healy's commission. Captain Healy would go on to become the commanding officer of the cutters Chandler, Corwin, Bear, McCulloch and Thetis, enforcing federal law along Alaska's entire coastline. For the last two decades of the 19th Century, Captain Healy was the U.S. Government in most of Alaska. A living legend, he served Alaska natives, merchant seamen and whaling crews

public domain photo

Captain Michael A. Healy

as friend, judge, doctor and policeman. He was also a whale rescuer. *(B-18-7-7)*

HENNING, JOHN F. "JACK" (1915-2009). Born in San Francisco, the son of Irish-Americans, Henning's maternal grandfather was a member of the Teamsters union and his father was a plumber and a charter member of the United Association of Journeymen Plumbers, Gas Fitters, Steam Fitters, and Steam Fitters' Helpers of the United States and Canada. Because of his work with the Association of Catholic Trade Unionists, Henning's father lost his job during the anti-union drives after World War I. Right out of St. Mary's College in Moraga in 1938, Henning joined his first union – the United Federal Workers. He later joined the Boilermakers Union and in 1949, became an aide to the head of the California Labor Federation. In the 1940s he was also active in the Irish Catholic fraternal organization, Knights of the Red Branch. He was a strong supporter of Irish republicanism, the Irish American Unity Conference and the Irish Northern Aid Committee. In 1945, he co-founded the Irish Literary and Historical Society. During the Kennedy and Johnson administrations, Henning served as Undersecretary of Labor. He was the U.S. Ambassador to New Zealand from 1967 to 1969. From 1970 until he retired in 1996, he was secretary treasurer of the California Labor Federation. Beginning in the 80s, Henning served a 12-year term as a UC regent. A close friend and ally of labor leader César Chávez, in 1975, Henning helped the United Farm Workers win passage of the landmark California Agricultural Labor Relations Act. In Henning's 1996 retirement speech from the state labor federation he said, "If by a suspension of the laws of nature, I were young again, I would follow no other course, no other flag but the flag of labor." *(U-3-7-2)*

HICKMAN, WILLIAM EDWARD "EDDIE" (1908-1928). Hickman moved to Los Angeles from Kansas City, Missouri right after high school. Hickman's senior year book lists him as Vice-President Senior Class, President Central Webster Club, Central Chapter National Honor Society and the list of accolades go on. His father had deserted the family and was so hated, that Hickman's mother listed herself as a widow in the 1926 Kansas City directory. On December 15, 1927 in Los Angeles, Hickman kidnapped the 12 year-old daughter of a banker and sent the young girl's father a ransom note. After meeting the ransom demands, Perry Parker was given his murdered daughter's remains. William Hickman was captured in Oregon. His sensational Los Angeles trial was covered by Edgar Rice Burroughs for the Los Angeles Examiner. On October 19, 1928, Hickman was executed by hanging at California's San Quentin State Prison. *(G-16-21-5)*

HIGGINS, EDWARD (1821-1875). The Civil War Confederate Brigadier General was born in Norfolk, Virginia, and raised in Louisiana. He was appointed a midshipman in the U.S. Navy in 1836. He served in the Navy during the Mexican-American War, and at its close, came to California where he served as second in command when the United States took possession of Monterey in 1847. He resigned as a Lieutenant in 1854 and headed to New York and entered the merchant marine where he stayed until it was evident that there would be war between the North and South. In the spring of 1861 he joined the 1st Louisiana Artillery as Captain. He was then promoted to Lieutenant Colonel of the 21st Louisiana Infantry. He went on to serve as the Colonel of the 22nd Louisiana Artillery. At the Confederate surrender of Vicksburg in July 1863, he became a prisoner.

However, he was exchanged and shortly thereafter was promoted to Brigadier General. After the War, he returned to New York and worked for an insurance company. Former New York employers from before the War recommended him for a job in San Francisco as the Agent of the Pacific Mail Company, which he took. He worked at that for a time before becoming a stockbroker. He died in San Francisco and left behind a wife and brother. He was originally buried in San Francisco's Calvary Cemetery and reinterred in Colma, following the complete removal of Calvary cemetery remains to Holy Cross in 1942. *(Calvary-12-3-17)*

HOFFER, ERIC (1902-1983). Born in the Bronx, Hoffer lost his sight from age 7 to 15, following a traumatic incident. With both his parents dead by the time he was 18, Hoffer took a bus to Los Angeles where he lived on skid row for 10 years, writing, reading and working odd jobs. In 1951, the self-educated longshoreman and philosopher penned his first book, The True Believer, which sold 500,000 copies and gave him quite a cult following. An American social writer, Hoffer authored ten books and was awarded the Presidential Medal of Freedom in February, 1983 by President Ronald Reagan. He died in his sleep three months later. *(St. Michael-7-7)*

KENDRICK, CHARLES (1876-1970). Born in San Francisco, necessity caused Kendrick to quit school at 12 and go to work. His good grades, however, allowed him early graduation. He worked seven days a week as a grocery boy. He was diligent, and his salary climbed. Still working, in 1892 he enrolled in Lincoln Night High School from which he graduated in 1895. With the encouragement of a teacher, he attended college at night. He then went on to study law at night school and graduated from the Kent Law School in 1898. Off to Petaluma he ventured, and became very successful in real estate. Hours after the 1906 earthquake, he returned to San Francisco and wrote a first-hand eye-witness account, a valued historic document still available. Kendrick volunteered for frontline duty in WWI, and advanced to the rank of Major. He served at the Battle of Verdun and was awarded the Purple Heart and Silver Star for bravery under fire. In addition, the French made him a member of the Legion of Honor. When he returned from the First World War, he was instrumental in the creation of San Francisco's War Memorial Complex. In 1927, he built San Francisco's Schlage Lock Company into a world leader. (The company sold in 1974 for $84 million.) He helped establish the Hetch Hetchy Water System. He was a member of the City Planning Commission, 1931-1934. During the Great Depression he served on the San Francisco Relief Committee and during WWII, he served on the War Production Board. A humble man, he was a benefactor to many. Perhaps his hardest and greatest personal achievement was the dangerous and nearly impossible, self-given task to retrieve the remains of his son, Lt. Charles Warren Kendrick, who was killed in action October 2, 1942 in the Battle of Guadalcanal. The Marine fighter pilot's father was successful. His book, Memoirs of Charles Kendrick, published by his wife in 1972 is an extraordinary read. *(Mausoleum-4-PS-1-3)*

McCARTHY, LEO T. (1930-2007). Born in Auckland, New Zealand, McCarthy immigrated with his parents to California when he was three. The family – his parents and his three older brothers moved to a flat in San Francisco's Mission District on 19th Street between Guerrero and Dolores streets. His father would go on to own and run the bar, McCarthy's Big Glass, on Mission Street. McCarthy attended Saint Ignatius College Preparatory in San Francisco, received his B.A. in history from the University of San Francisco and graduated from San Francisco Law School. During the Korean War, McCarthy served in the United States Air Force from 1951-1952 in the intelligence unit of the Strategic Air Command. In 1958, McCarthy managed the successful campaign for State Senate of John Eugene McAteer and afterwards served as McActeer's Administrative Assistant. In 1963, at age 33, McCarthy won a seat on the San Francisco Board of Supervisors. In 1968 he was elected to the State Assembly where he went on to serve as Speaker of the Assembly from 1974 to 1980. Beginning in 1982, McCarthy served three consecutive four-year terms as the Lieutenant Governor of California. Throughout his life he remained a "champion of Democratic causes and underdog constituencies, including the environment, healthcare and education." *(H-68A-18)*

McEACHERN, JAMES M. (1881-1969). A native of Prince Edward Island, Canada, McEachern moved to San Francisco as a young man. He joined the San Francisco Police Department in 1908 and wore Badge No. 204 until his retirement in 1948. In 1920, he competed in the Summer Olympics held in Antwerp and finished eighth in the 16-pound hammer throw competition and tenth in the 56-pound weight throw event. Four years later at the Summer Olympics in Paris, he finished sixth in the hammer throw competition. The San Francisco Chronicle wrote this about the police officer, and strong man, in 1934, "His powerful arms and ability to juggle the toughest like so much paper make him a one-man crime prevention unit." *(Mausoleum-7-219)*

McLAUGHLIN, KENNETH P. (1912-1966). The son of an undertaker, McLaughlin was born and raised in San Francisco's Mission District. He joined the San Francisco Chronicle in 1936 after working for International News Photos and the Call-Bulletin. During the Second World War he spent 21 months in China as a broadcaster and as a photographer for the Office of War Information. The third president of the National Press Photographers Association, McLaughlin was the recipient of many awards. He was a photographer for the San Francisco Chronicle until his death in 1966. The NPPA has since named their coveted "Award of Merit" after him. *(5-2-60)*

MOLERA, ANDREW. (1897-1931). The grandson of Juan Bautista Rogers Cooper, Molera owned eight square miles of land in Castroville, California (Monterey County). He had rented out his farming land to sugar beet growers for quite a number of years. But in the 1920s, Molera decided to lease the land to any farmer willing to try and grow artichokes, which he believed would be a profitable crop. Molera's "artichoke" vision proved correct. By 1929, artichokes were the third largest cash crop in the Salinas Valley. When Molera died, at age 34, his estate passed to his sister Frances and remained in her care until her death. She donated the 4,766 acres to the state of California and it is now the Andrew Molera State Park, the largest state park on the Big Sur coast. *(I-4-2-4)*

MONTGOMERY, JOHN J. (1858-1911). Born in a house on B Street in Yuba City, CA, Montgomery was an aviation pioneer. In 1864, his family moved to Oakland and on July 2, 1869, Montgomery saw Frederick Marriott's exhibition flight of his twenty-eight foot model steam-driven airship, "Flying Avitor," the first powered flying machine. From then on Montgomery studied birds in flights and made early "flying" machine models. He studied physics at St. Ignatius College in San Francisco and graduated with a MS in Science in 1880. He set up a lab in Otay Mesa (San Diego), and built his first airplanes with the aid of his sister Jane Montgomery. In August of 1883, he flew his gull-winged airplane which was the "first controlled flight of man in a heavier than aircraft." In 1893, he attended the Aeronautical Congress, Conference on Aerial Navigation at the World Fair in Chicago and presented his paper "Soaring Flight." He received his Ph.D. from Santa Clara College in 1901. Among his continued projects, he experimented with 4 and 8 foot wingspread models. With pilot Daniel Maloney, he held several exhibitions where planes were raised 500 to 4,000 feet by a hot air balloon, then released and flown to the ground. In a 1911 gliding experiment, Montgomery made a slight alteration in his flying pattern. Freakishly, this resulted in a protruding stove-bolt striking him with a fatal, penetrating force behind his ear. His wife, Regina "Cleary" Montgomery buried him in her family's plot at Holy Cross. *(E-9-3-3)*

MOSCONE, GEORGE R. (1929-1978). Born in San Francisco, Moscone attended St. Ignatius College Preparatory where he was an all-city basketball star. He attended the University of the Pacific on a basketball scholarship and he earned his J.D. from UC Hastings College of the Law. After serving in the United States Navy, Moscone started private practice in 1956. In 1963, Moscone won a seat on the San Francisco Board of Supervisors. In 1966, Moscone ran for and was elected to a seat in the California State Senate, representing the 10th District in San Francisco County. He served in the State Senate until becoming San Francisco's 37th mayor in January of 1976. Shortly after taking office, Moscone appointed Harvey Milk to the Board of Permit Appeals, making Milk the first openly gay city commissioner in the U.S. On November 27, 1978, Mayor Moscone along with San Francisco Supervisor Harvey Milk was assassinated at City Hall by San Francisco Supervisor Dan White. Mayor George Moscone's funeral procession to Holy Cross was accompanied by a 70-car, police escort. *(St. Michael-22-42)*

MUSTO, JOSEPH (1829-1904). Born in Genoa, Italy, Musto was a fifth-generation stone cutter and tile setter. At age 21, he headed to New York where he married Maria Sturla, also born and raised in Italy. Prior to coming to this country, Musto had fought in the military guard of King Carlo Alberto in the 1849 Battle of Novara. In 1851 or '52, he and Maria headed to California where Musto worked in the gold-mining camps in Sandy Gulch. Successful in his mining operations, he established a general store in Virginia City. A few years down the road, he and his brother Giovanni established a marble-manufacturing enterprise in San Francisco under the name Musto Brothers. In 1868, his business became Musto Steam Marble Co. The Musto Company's acclaimed marble work can be found at such local landmarks as the California Palace of the Legion of Honor, the San Francisco Opera

House and San Francisco City Hall. Joseph and his wife Maria had seven children. Their eldest, daughter Emilia Musto Tojetti, was the founder of the music department of the San Francisco Library. Their sons Clarence and Guido, and their daughter Carlotta's husband, J.B. Keenan, carried on in the family business which became Musto-Keenan Company in 1949, and which "gained a reputation for making top quality diamond tools to cut marble and tile more efficiently." The company is now known as MK Diamond. *(E-4-2-1-2)*

NOLAN, JOHN IGNATIUS (1874-1922). Born in San Francisco, Nolan worked as an iron molder. In 1911, he was elected to San Francisco's Board of Supervisors. In 1912, he served as secretary of the San Francisco Labor Council. In 1913, Nolan was elected to the 63rd United States Congress. A member of the Molder's Union, Nolan was the first labor congressman. He served four consecutive terms in Congress, and died not long after being reelected in 1922. Following his death, his wife Mae Nolan was elected to his Congressional seat. *(I-38-6)*

PHELAN, JAMES D. (1861-1930). Following the San Francisco Earthquake of 1906, this former Mayor of San Francisco gave $1,000,000 for the relief of the sufferers, the largest sum given by an individual. Born in San Francisco, Phelan was the son of an Irish immigrant who became a millionaire during the Gold Rush as a pioneer banker and capitalist. The well-educated Phelan, graduated with a law degree from the University of California, Berkeley. Following graduation, he went into the banking business, becoming a partner in Phelan & Son. Beginning in 1897, Phelan stepped into politics and served as San Francisco's mayor through 1901. Following the 1906 earthquake and by appointment of President Theodore Roosevelt, Phelan became Chairman of the Board of Directors of the San Francisco Relief and Red Cross Funds, thus

public domain photo
James D. Phelan

keeping the money out of the corrupt hands of San Francisco's Mayor Eugene Schmitz and Schmitz's crony, Abe Ruef. In the immediate aftermath of the earthquake, Phelan was an enthusiastic advocate of the plan to relocate Chinatown to Hunters Point. Phelan served as a U.S. Senator from 1915-1921. A generous supporter of the arts, Phelan hosted many literary events at his Villa Montalvo home in Saratoga. After his death, the estate was gifted to the people of Santa Clara County. It serves as a center for the performing and visual arts. *(D-1-2-1/4-OGV)*

ROSSI, PIETRO CARLO "PETER C" (1855-1911). In 1887, a vintage failed at Italian Swiss Colony (Sonoma, California) and Andrea Sbarboro, the Colony's founder, hired Rossi to assume the duties of Colony winemaker and chemist. Rossi, born in Dogliani, Italy, was from a long line of winemakers. He had a degree in agricultural chemistry from the University of Torino where he graduated with honors in 1875. Rossi accepted Sbarboro's job offer and took over as winemaker. By the late 1800s, the winery was producing 2 million gallons of wine per year, a volume becoming unmanageable using traditional winemaking techniques. The solution? Rossi pioneered temperature-controlled fermentation. Rossi married Amelie Caire, the daughter of Justinian Caire (of Santa Cruz Island fame), and they had 10 children. *(D-9-1-1/4-OGV)*

SBARBORO, ANDREA (1839-1923). Born in Acero, Genoa, Italy, Sbarboro came to New York with his parents in 1842. In 1852, at age 13, he traveled by ship with a family friend to San Francisco to work as a bookkeeper for his older brother Bartolomeo who was established in the grocery business. For many years the brothers worked at their store on Washington Street. Eventually, with his own growing family, Sbarboro ventured into the cooperative loan association business and then into the corporate world. Sbarboro would go on to establish a garbage disposal firm in San Francisco, as well as the Italian American Bank and the Italian Swiss Agricultural Colony. In regards to the latter, in 1881 Sbarboro moved to northern Sonoma where he established two communities in the Alexander Valley, Asti and Chianti, as part of his Italian Swiss Agricultural Colony. It was there that Sbarboro became one of the winemaking pioneers of California. *(E-17-1)*

SCHMITZ, EUGENE E. (1864-1928). Born in San Francisco, Schmitz was a violinist. He was at one point the orchestra leader for the very fashionable Columbia Theatre on Powell Street. Additionally, he was President of the Musicians' Union. His nickname was "Handsome Gene" and in 1901, he was chosen by attorney and notorious political boss Abraham Ruef to run for Mayor of San Francisco and won under Ruef's newly formed Union Labor Party. On January 8, 1902, Eugene Schmitz became the 26th Mayor of San Francisco. On the day of the Great San Francisco Earthquake, Wednesday, April 18, 1906, Schmitz formed a Committee of 50 prominent citizens which included businessmen, politicians, religious leaders and civic leaders to help manage the crisis. On April 18, Schmitz also issued his infamous proclamation: "The Federal Troops, the members of the Regular Police Force and

public domain photo

Eugene E. Schmitz

33

all Special Police Officers have been authorized by me to KILL any and all persons found engaged in Looting or in the Commission of Any Other Crime." After the earthquake and fire, Mayor Eugene Schmitz was indicted and convicted on 27 counts of graft and corruption. Found guilty of extortion in June of '07, the office of the Mayor was declared vacant while Schmitz waited out his appeal in San Francisco County Jail. An appeals court reversed his conviction, and Schmitz was later elected to the Board of Supervisors. *(B-3-11-8)*

SHAUGHNESSY, PATRICK H. (1852-1925). From the 1906 pages of the Fire and Water Engineering journal, the Merchants Association of San Francisco reported the following on the Virginia born, San Francisco firefighter. "Patrick H. Shaughnessy entered the fire department of San Francisco as a hoseman of engine company No. 9 in 1885, and served in that capacity for one year." One year later, Shaughnessy was appointed foreman of the same engine company. "In 1890 he was raised to the rank of battalion chief, and ten years afterward to that of second assistant chief." Following the death of SFFD Chief Dennis Sullivan, who was killed as a result of the 1906 earthquake, Shaughnessy was appointed SFFD Chief Engineer on June 16, 1906. "Chief Shaughnessy's record in the department is that of great personal bravery," the Merchants write. "As a life saver, he won the highest fame and received from the Merchants' association a special medal for his heroic rescue of a woman, whom he carried on his back from the top floor of the burning Baldwin hotel, (amid the fire and smoke), bringing her down to safety." Under Shaughnessy's leadership, construction was initiated on the installation of the Auxiliary Water Supply System, considered the most important protective feature of the San Francisco Fire Department. He retired from the department on March 16, 1910. *(I-30-3)*

SMITH, JAMES FRANCIS (1859-1928). Born in San Francisco, Smith attended Santa Clara College and Hastings College of Law then headed off to work for a San Francisco law firm. A captain in the National Guard, he along with five others founded The Young Men's Institute in San Francisco, a Catholic fraternal organization, on March 4, 1883. When the Spanish-American War began in 1898, he was made a Colonel of the First California Regiment, United States Volunteers. He served with Theodore Roosevelt in the Rough Riders and his regiment took part in the Battle of Manila. In 1899 he was promoted to brigadier general. In July of 1899 he was made military governor of Negros Island. In 1901 he was appointed Associate Justice of the Supreme Court of the Philippines. In 1906, he was made Governor-General of the Islands. In 1909, the Honorable James F. Smith was appointed by President Taft to the U.S. Court of Customs Appeals in Washington, D.C. where he served until his death. There is a plaque in honor of (Colonel) James F. Smith located at Camp Merriam,

public domain photo

James Francis Smith

San Francisco. This is on the eastern border of the Presidio, close to the Lombard Gate. The camp was named for Brigadier General Henry Merriam, and it was where the First California Volunteer Infantry camped while awaiting transport to the Philippines. *(E-10-6-4)*

SMITH, MACDONALD "MAC" (1890-1949). One of the top golfers in the world, Smith was born in Carnoustie, Scotland, in the council area of Angus. He was the son of a greenskeeper and learned the game, along with his famous golfing brothers, on the legendary and difficult Carnoustie Golf Links. He emigrated to Northern California with his parents in 1908. His goal was to seek golf opportunities. While he won 24 times on the early PGA Tour, and won the Western Open three times (1912, 1925 and 1933), he is nevertheless considered the greatest golfer who never won a major championship. Records show he finished second in the 1930 US Open and second in the 1930 and 1932 British Opens. He finished within three shots of the winner in five US Opens (1910, 1913, 1930, 1934 and 1936) and six British Opens (1923, 1924, 1925, 1930, 1931 and 1932). Noted for his beautiful swing, from the Sports Illustrated magazine vault, observers reported that when studying "slow-motion pictures of Mac's swing under the strain of the big events, he had a tendency to come into the ball with a slightly closed club face." He was inducted into the P.G.A. Golf Hall of Fame in 1954 and in 1990, he was inducted into the World Golf Hall of Fame. *(D-5-8-4)*

SULLIVAN, DENNIS T. (1852-1906). On April 22, 1906, Dennis Sullivan, Chief Engineer of the San Francisco Fire Department, died from injuries sustained during the earthquake of April 18, 1906. Born in Florence, New Jersey, Sullivan grew up in Utica, New York, where he learned the trade of a carriage blacksmith. For several years he was a member of Utica's Empire and Eagle Hose Company No. 4. In 1874, he headed to San Francisco following the death of his parents. At age 25, he entered the SFFD as a hoseman of engine company No. 3. Sullivan rose rapidly through the ranks and was appointed Assistant Chief Engineer in February of 1890. In March of 1893 he was appointed SFFD Chief Engineer. His leadership was recognized for bringing the Fire Department to its very highest standard of efficiency. As far back as 1891, he advocated for the establishment of an auxiliary high pressure salt water supply for the City. Had it been in effect when the horrific conflagration following the earthquake took place, it would have saved lives and property. On April 18, 1906, the dome of the California Theatre and Hotel crashed through the fire station in which Sullivan was living. Asleep at the time, Chief Sullivan ran to save his wife and fell through an opening made by the falling tower. The beloved Fire Chief died four days later. San Francisco Landmark #42, 870 Bush Street, between Mason and Taylor, is dedicated to Chief Sullivan. It reads – "By fire shall hearts be proven, lest virtue's gold grow dim, and his life by fire was tested, in life's ordeal of him. Now California renders, the laurels that he won – 'dead on the field of honor,' her hero and her son." *(I-21-33)*

TOBIN, CYRIL R. (1880-1977). Cyril is the son of Robert Tobin and grandson of Richard Tobin, co-founder of Hibernia Bank. When his uncle Joseph died in 1918, Cyril took over the firm of Tobin & Tobin, additionally founded by his grandfather Richard Tobin. An original member of the 1927-founded St. Francis Yacht Club, where Cyril would serve as Commodore in 1934, he has a long and storied history with many beautiful sailing vessels including the 72' Marconi-rigged schooner "Seaweed," which was borrowed by the U.S. Navy to serve in the Second World War. (The Navy did not have enough patrol boats to send to sea as early warning scouts – should the Japanese Navy come to the West Coast.) Seaweed's oiled teak decks and beautiful varnish were painted over in standard Navy grey. She served her time proudly but it took a year to get her back to "yacht" condition and some of the grey paint could never be removed. Cyril also served as owner and president of Hibernia Bank. *(D-11-9-3-7)*

TOBIN, JOSEPH SADOC (1868-1918). Born in San Francisco, and one of the four sons of Hibernia Bank co-founder Richard Tobin, Joseph was named after San Francisco's first Archbishop Joseph Sadoc Alemany, a very dear friend of his father's. Joseph graduated with distinction from Georgetown University in 1890. In 1892 he achieved his law degree from Georgetown and was also admitted to the California Bar. He would eventually become the head of the law department in Hibernia Bank. He was elected to San Francisco's Board of Supervisors and served from 1900 to 1902. He served on the Committee of Fifty which was called into existence by San Francisco Mayor Eugene Schmitz following the 1906 earthquake. He also served on the board of the 1915 Panama Pacific Exposition. *(D-11-9-4-3)*

TOBIN, RICHARD (1832-1887). Born in County Tipperary, Ireland, Richard was brought to Chile by his parents when he was a child. He became proficient in Spanish and French. He was secretary to Archbishop Alemany in San Francisco before studying law and after achieving his law degree, he served as Archbishop Alemany's legal advisor. In 1852, he founded the law firm Tobin & Tobin. Tobin & Tobin is California's oldest law firm. In 1859, he co-founded Hibernia Savings and Loan Society with his brother Robert J. Tobin. He was additionally the man behind the 10-foot wide, 10-foot high and 90-foot long tunnel blasted through the promontory by Mussel Rock, a "greenstone assemblage" offshore from Daly City at the Pacific Ocean. Richard's goal was to provide a better route for his buggy, riding back and forth between his family's San Francisco home and their house in Rockaway Beach, Pacifica. Built in 1875 and a disaster from the get-go, Tobin was only able to use the tunnel three times before it was taken back by the ocean. It was referred to as "Tobin's Folly" and what remained of it was completely destroyed in the 1906 earthquake. *(D-11-9-3-1)*

TOBIN, ROBERT J. (born 1827). Born in County Tipperary, Ireland, Robert moved with his family to Valparaiso, Chile in 1843. He met and married his wife there. When the United States acquired California in 1846, Tobin and his wife set off for this "new" land and arrived in Yerba Buena in 1846. (Yerba Buena became San Francisco in 1847.) Robert was immediately successful in business and was able to purchase a lot which became the southwest corner of Pacific and Montgomery Streets. When gold was discovered, he headed off for a short time to the American River. He studied law and when he returned to San Francisco he was elected City Judge. He was on the bench in 1859 when he and his brother founded Hibernia Savings and Loan Society. He was named police commissioner by Governor William Irwin in 1878 and served on the commission until 1900. *(D-11-9-3-3)*

Sister Dolores Armer

THOSE WHO HAVE DEDICATED THEIR LIVES
TO GOD AND NEIGHBOR

"Go to the people. Learn from them. Live with them.
Start with what they know. Build with what they have.
The best of leaders when the job is done,
when the task is accomplished, the people will say
we have done it ourselves."
~ Laozi, legendary founder of philosophical Taoism

There are many who have served in faith and who are buried at Holy Cross.
This book introduces six.

Women of Faith

ARMER, SISTER M. DOLORES (SHF) (1851-1905): Born in Sydney, Australia, Lizzie Armer arrived in San Francisco with her parents and two brothers when she was very young. Shortly after their arrival, Lizzie's mother died and her father, Robert Armer, entrusted her to the care of Richard and Mary Tobin who raised Lizzie with their own children. The Tobin's were a devout Catholic family and Lizzie was very drawn to Catholicism. Originally baptized Anglican, with her father's permission she was received into the Catholic Church. Lizzie was deeply religious and as a teen, she would teach young "waifs" about God. She planned to become a Carmelite nun but Archbishop Alemany suggested she instead care for those children whose mothers had to work. From this advice in 1872, the young woman co-founded, along with Father John Prendergast, the Congregation of the Sisters of the Holy Family, a community of Roman Catholic Sisters in San Francisco. Father Prendergast told the young Sister, who was barely past twenty, to: "help those people, no matter their religion, who are falling through the cracks." The Sisters devoted their work to broken families, the poor, the hungry, the aged and the sick with special focus on teaching religion to children and caring for children who otherwise would have no care. In 1878, Sister Dolores opened the first Day Home to "provide a place where the needs of the child could be attended to while peace of mind and material assistance" could be offered to struggling, overwhelmed parents. In 1880, Sister Dolores became Mother General of the Holy Family Order. When "Lizzie" died at the early age of 54, Mary Tobin, who had always considered Mother Dolores an elder daughter, provided the casket "of broadcloth, trimmed with oxidized silver," and the pall was composed of lilies of the valley. The congregation of the Sisters of the Holy Family is the only religious community of women founded in the United States west of the Mississippi. *(XG-4-10)*

McGRATH, SISTER FREDERICA (DC) (1825-1913). Born as Alice Eliza McGrath in Tipperary County, Ireland, Alice arrived in Philadelphia with her parents when she was ten. At age 18, she joined Mother Seton's Sisters of Charity in Emmitsburg, Maryland. She spent a number of years teaching in Catholic schools along the East Coast before being called to serve in San Francisco. There she became principal of St. Vincent's Boy's School. In 1859, the Comstock Lode (silver) was discovered in Virginia City, Nevada. Parents were orphaning children in their efforts to strike it rich. In 1864, the Archdiocese of San Francisco sent three nuns – Sisters Frederica, Xavier and Mary Elizabeth to help the children. Under very difficult living and working conditions, the three Sisters opened St. Mary's School and Asylum in 1864 and St. Marie Louise Hospital in 1875. Ignoring what could prove to be problematic religious differences, Sister McGrath found an Episcopalian physician to provide free medical care for the orphaned children. She also talked the State of Nevada into financing the Nevada Children's Asylum in 1867. When state support was pulled in 1870, due to a public outcry on the need of church and state to remain separate, Sister Frederica rolled up her sleeves and approached others, including John and Mary Mackay, partners in the Comstock Mine, to lend a very big helping hand. Astutely, Sister Frederica publicly thanked donors via the newspaper, which included listing their donation. Sister Frederica's charity and good works became known throughout the state and many traveled hundreds of miles to seek her counsel. "Her solid piety, close union to God, and childlike devotion to the Blessed Mother was immediately apparent to youthful eyes, and strongly influenced anyone she contacted." (Quote attributed to miners who knew her.) After 22 years of service, and with the heyday of silver mining a thing of the past, Sister Frederica returned to San Francisco where she lived the remainder of her days. *(XC-9-17)*

RUSSELL, SISTER MARY BAPTIST (RSM) (1829-1898). Born in Newry, Ireland, Katherine Russell was the third child of Arthur and Margaret Russell. Her family was able to provide their children with the best education possible and Katherine's love for the importance of education was life long. In the summer of 1845, a potato blight arrived in Ireland destroying 50 percent of what was expected to be a bumper crop. This natural catastrophe set off Ireland's Great Famine (1845-1852) and Katherine gave of her time and her heart to help those in need and she discovered her vocation. In November of 1848, Katherine entered the order of the Sisters of Mercy in Kinsale, Ireland, and it was not long thereafter that the postulant worked with victims of the cholera epidemic brought on by the famine crisis. In 1849, Katherine received the habit of a Sister of Mercy and the religious name of Sister Mary Baptist. In 1851 she made her final profession of vows and for the next three years, taught at the convent school. When Father Hugh Gallagher, a delegate of San Francisco's first Archbishop Joseph Alemany arrived at Kinsale seeking "apostles" for the West, he described such a picture of lawlessness that no one wanted to go. But then many in the religious community stepped up to volunteer and in 1854, the 25-year-old Sister of Mercy from Newry was appointed superior of the eight sisters chosen to start the mission out West. The harsh trip took several months and when the eight sisters arrived, not only were they not greeted with any fanfare or a place to stay, an anti-Catholic newspaper wrote they should leave San Francisco immediately. Startled but undaunted, under Mother Mary Baptist's sturdy guidance the sisters rented a house on the 600 block of Vallejo Street and their work began. They visited the sick in a nearby hospital, they opened a night school for adults and they established a shelter for unemployed women. In 1855, a cholera epidemic arrived in San Francisco by way of ship. Mother Baptist offered San Francisco city officials her considerable experience working with cholera victims and they accepted with relief. The sisters were then asked to staff all of San Francisco's hospitals. Mother Mary Baptist was also gifted with good business acumen and she opened St. Mary's Hospital in July of 1857.

photo www.mercyburl.org
Sister Mary Baptist Russell

(Relocated in 1905 by the Sisters of Mercy, St. Mary's Medical Center is the oldest continually operating hospital in San Francisco and the first Catholic hospital west of the Rockies.) Under Mother Mary Baptist's guidance, the pioneer sisters would additionally open, among other charitable institutions – a home for widows, an orphanage and the Magdalene Asylum (to assist and reeducate prostitutes). She established a program for the Sisters of Mercy to visit and minister to inmates in the city prison, the county jail and San Quentin State Prison, including those on death row. In addition, the Sisters of Mercy comforted the sick and dying, worked with the poor and the aged, and as their numbers grew larger, they went into Sacramento and Grass Valley, establishing other like nonprofits to help those in need. Mother Mary Baptist died at St. Mary's Hospital in 1898. She was buried at St. Michael's Cemetery next to the Magdalene Asylum. In her obituary, the San Francisco Bulletin called her the "best-known charitable worker on the Pacific Coast." In recognition of her heroic work, the city of San Francisco granted free public transport to all religious; a privilege which is still honored. In 1931, Mother Mary Baptist, along with more than 50 other Sisters of Mercy buried at St. Michael's, was reinterred at Holy Cross. *(XD-7-9/10)*

Men of Faith

Priest Plot

Jean Bartlett photo

HESLIN, FATHER PATRICK (1863-1921). It was a foggy evening on August 2, 1921, when Irish born, 58-year-old Father Patrick Heslin, serving as pastor of Holy Angels Church in Colma, heard a knock at the rectory door. Housekeeper Maria Wendell and neighbor Mary Bianchi would later report that the man knocking wore goggles and a heavy overcoat, with the collar of his coat pulled up high to conceal his face. The man told Father Heslin that he was needed to minister to a "dying friend" in Salada Beach (now Pacifica). Moments later Father Patrick, dressed in cleric apparel, climbed into the front seat of William Hightower's touring car. When Father Heslin didn't return, the housekeeper phoned the police. The next day, a ransom note was delivered to Holy Angels and the church offered a reward of $6,500 to anyone who could provide information on Father Heslin's whereabouts. On August 10, William A. Hightower, age 41, showed up to collect the reward. He told the police that some woman had told him that some man had shot and buried a man at the bottom of a sand cliff, on the beach, just over the hill. Suspicious, the police accompanied Hightower to this beach location. With shovel in hand, Hightower dug two feet in. When the police told him to be careful because he might strike the buried man's face with the shovel, Hightower told them not to worry; he was digging near the priest's feet. Hightower, an unemployed master baker originally from Texas, was convicted of Heslin's murder and served 44 years in prison. He was paroled in 1965 at age 86. *(Priest Plot-B-4-3)*

Jean Bartlett photo

Rev. Patrick Heslin (1863-1921)

TOBIN, REVEREND JOHN P. (1876-1929). Born in Ireland, Father Tobin was ordained a priest in Baltimore in June of 1902. Shortly thereafter, he headed out to San Francisco where he served as assistant pastor of Mission Dolores for 14 years. On January 7, 1917, Archbishop Edward J.

Hanna established the new Parish of St. Cecilia in San Francisco, out in the "sand dunes" of the Parkside District. The boundaries of the parish extended from the Pacific Ocean on the west, to Twin Peaks on the east, and from Pacheco Street on the north to Balboa Terrace on the south. Father Tobin, who served as St. Cecilia's first pastor, first procured a two-story home as both rectory and church to serve the 59 families in the parish. With additional moves, expansions and remodels in between, in May of 1926, Father Tobin secured land for the ever-growing St. Cecilia Church, School, Convent and Rectory. (St. Cecilia is located today at 2555 17th Avenue, San Francisco.) While serving the needs of his parishioners, Father Tobin also devoted time to serving the needy at Laguna Honda Home in San Francisco. Opened in 1867, Laguna Honda was always a place to help those who didn't have – beginning with the individuals and families who did not strike it rich in the Gold Rush days. Following the 1906 earthquake, Laguna Honda became a relief home and by the 1920s it was a skilled nursing facility. Father Tobin ministered to the poor of Laguna Honda, which included the comfort of a Christian burial. He called those he served at Laguna Honda, his "dear friends." Father Tobin died on Good Friday morning, March 29, 1929. Per his request, he was buried with his dear friends in "Potter's" Field, here at Holy Cross. *(A-29-80)*

YORKE, FATHER PETER C. (WARRIOR PRIEST) (1864-1925). Born in County Galway, Ireland, Father Yorke was a priest, an educator, an editor, and an unrestrained, knowledgeable verbal combatant who championed that the Irish-American working man be allowed the right to "economic and religious" security. He was a labor priest. He was an Irish patriot. He was a liturgist and author. He was one of the key leaders of the Irish nationalist community in the United States in the twentieth century. Peter was the youngest child of Gregory and Brigid Yorke. His father, a sea captain, died six months before he was born. In 1882 he entered the seminary at Maynooth to prepare for the priesthood. He did not wish to remain in Ireland under British rule and was transferred to St. Mary's Seminary in Baltimore. In 1887, he was ordained by Cardinal Joseph Gibbons and subsequently moved to San Francisco to begin his ministry. In 1894, he was appointed chancellor and secretary to Archbishop Patrick W. Riordan. He was also appointed as editor of the Archdiocesan newspaper, The Monitor. In 1901, Father Yorke became involved in the San Francisco waterfront strike, placing the Church in San Francisco firmly on the side of labor. He pointed out that as a priest, "My duty is with workingmen, who are struggling for their rights because that is the historical position of the priesthood and because that is the Lord's command." In 1902, he founded and edited a local newspaper called The Leader, which defended both the rights of labor and Irish nationalism. The Leader was a point of contention between Father Yorke and Archbishop Riordan and in 1909, Father Yorke stepped down as editor, though "unofficially" continued to weigh in with his opinions. Father Yorke sided with the Union Labor Party during the prosecution of corrupt city officials. He became president of the National Catholic Educational Association and he served as regent of the University of California at Berkeley. He wrote eight books. He championed Irish independence from England and raised more than $40,000 for the Irish Relief Fund, set up to aid orphans, families and dependents of imprisoned participants in the Easter Week uprising against British rule. Peter Yorke died on Palm Sunday, April 5, 1925 at 10:45 in the morning. He was buried at Holy Cross. In all the years since and continuing, the United Irish Societies of San Francisco and Holy Cross have invited the public to join them on Palm Sunday for their annual Mass honoring the Irish-American priest and union labor leader. The Mass is celebrated at All Saints Mausoleum Chapel and following the service, a fife and drum band leads the procession to where Father Yorke's cross-shaped sarcophagus waits quietly on the green. *(1-22-9-3)*

Holy Cross photo

Father Peter Yorke

REMBRANCE *Of* INFANTS AND CHILDREN

Jean Bartlett photo

The Children's Perpetual Care Section of Holy Cross Catholic Cemetery

*"There is something you must always remember.
You are braver than you believe, stronger than you seem,
and smarter than you think."
~ A.A. Milne's Christopher Robin to Winnie the Pooh.*

From atop the gently sloping green of Holy Cross's Section X, there are several columns of headstones, each bearing the name of a postulant, an abbess, a sister, a mother superior. In fact, included among the women religious, is a monument to Sister M. Dolores Armer, who like her sisters in faith, devoted her life to the care of young ones. How fitting that the view from where these women now rest, looks out to the memorials of children.

Among the children's gravesites, many which are colored by balloons, fresh flowers, stuffed animals and ribbons, there are memorial portraits on some of the stones. These oval photographs, tinted by brush and remembrance – look out to anyone who strolls among the peaceful setting. "Don't forget me."

Jean Bartlett photo

"The best and most beautiful things in the world cannot be seen, nor touched, but are felt in the heart." ~ Helen Keller.

Statue of Rachel Mourning

Here in Section W, are infants lost at birth. Sometimes their family had little money and their child was buried here for free. Sometimes to spare the grieving mother, the hospital would arrange for her child to be interred here. It seems there was a time in the mid-20th century when too many women were unable to say goodbye to their tiny angel, and often this is a place of comfort for women now in their elder years. The statue of Rachel Mourning reads: "Mourning our babies who died before, at, or soon after birth. We hold these, our children gently in our hearts and pray for all who mourn them."

"A voice was heard in Rama, weeping and loud lamentation;
Rachel weeping for her children, and she would not be comforted,
because they are no more." (Matt. 2:18)

47

Wall relief by Fila Raventos, All Saints Mausoleum Chapel

NOTABLE BUILDINGS

All Saints Mausoleum

All Saints Mausoleum was designed by Denis Shanagher and constructed by Frank Portman Company. Dedication ceremonies were held on Memorial Day in 1988. Near the entrance to the Mausoleum, is a bronze sculpture "All Saints" by local artist Rosa Estabenez. Inside, the chapel there is a wall relief by Fila Raventos. It depicts the Saints (St. Thomas More, St. Anthony, St. Joseph, St. Patrick, St. Bernadette, St. Anne, St. Joan of Arc and Mother Seton) waiting in welcome at the gates of heaven. The stained glass windows and skylights in the chapel were crafted by Wallach Studios and were chosen to emphasize the details of the relief. The marble throughout the Mausoleum was imported from Spain, Portugal and Italy. Each of the corridors in the Mausoleum is named after a Saint who is depicted in a stained glass window at the end of the corridor. All Saints Mausoleum was designed to be expanded to three stories allowing a total capacity of 43,000 entombments. Each year on Palm Sunday, Holy Cross Catholic Cemetery and the United Irish Societies of San Francisco honor Irish-American, union labor priest Father Peter Yorke, with a celebratory mass at All Saints, which is followed with a procession to his gravesite. In addition, on the first Saturday of every month, All Saints Mausoleum Chapel celebrates mass at 11:00 a.m., offered for all those interred in the cemetery.

Holy Cross Mausoleum

The classical-style Holy Cross Mausoleum was designed by artisan John McQuarrie and dedicated in 1921 by Archbishop Edward Joseph Hanna. McQuarrie's bronze work and

Jean Bartlett photo

Holy Cross Mausoleum

marble friezes are visible throughout the building. McQuarrie, a native San Franciscan who worked in a variety of media including bronze, poured stone, stained glass, painting, architectural design and textile, created many renowned works of art which include the Golden Spike in the Union Pacific Depot in Salt Lake City, Utah, the Donner Party Monument at Donner Lake, California, the Southern Pacific Sacramento Depot Mural and the Bear Flag Monument in Sonoma, California. The Mausoleum originally covered a four-acre area and contained 14,000 crypts. Since 1921, 10 additions have been added to the original structure and the Mausoleum now covers eight acres, and the number of crypts in the building have grown to 38,500. The last addition, Gallery of the Ascension, was completed in 1977. The sepulcher of Archbishop Joseph Sadoc Alemany is located in the central apse which is reserved for the burial of the archbishops of San Francisco. The marble in the rotunda is primarily French rouge antique. (The story goes that the marble was ordered from France and loaded at the dock for transport to San Francisco. As it turns out, the purchased marble was considered a National treasure by the French Government, and had they known, they would never have approved of its sale. Too late! The ship had already sailed and Holy Cross was not giving it back.) Along with San Francisco's archbishops, the Mausoleum is home to many famous residents including William S. O'Brien - one of the four Comstock silver kings; Angelo J. Rossi - 31st Mayor of San Francisco, appointed by resigning Mayor James Rolph; Michael Geraldi - opened the first restaurant in San Francisco's Fisherman's Wharf, Fisherman's Grotto No. 9, in 1935; and restaurateur Agostino Giuntoli - owner of the world-famous Bimbo's 365 Club which he opened in San Francisco in 1931 as a Prohibition-era speakeasy. A walk through the Mausoleum reveals stained glass windows, statues and a number of private rooms that are gated. Holy Cross Mausoleum made its brief film debut, and its only film role to date, in the 1971 cult classic "Harold and Maude."

The Receiving Chapel

Designed by San Francisco architect Frank W. Trabucco, the Receiving Chapel was completed in 1963. It contains five chapels which allow five services to be conducted simultaneously without one interfering with the other. Within each chapel, behind its respective altar of French rouge antique and Pernice Pastello marble (framed by stained Philippine mahogany), is an oil painting of

Holy Cross photo
Holy Cross Receiving Chapel 1962

Holy Cross Receiving Chapel 2012

one of the five Glorious Mysteries – The Resurrection, The Ascension, The Holy Spirit, The Assumption and The Coronation. These murals, 19 feet high and nine feet wide, were painted by Thomas Lawless of San Francisco. The floors are of terrazzo marble and each altar front contains four stainless steel sliding doors that cover four crypts. The Chapel can accommodate 50 funerals per day and twenty caskets can be stored in the crypts of the five altars at one time. Hydraulic tables allow the placement of each casket to be brought into the chapel from the hearse, and back into the hearse again for delivery to the gravesite. The five chapels fan out in a circular fashion from a hexagonal shaped room called the receiving center. Upper and lower roofs of the chapel consist of two levels of thin concrete taped vaults set in 30 identical bays around a circular plan. From the roof, a 40-foot steel tower, finished in blue enamel, rises towards the heavens.

MONUMENTS,
STATUES AND MEMORIALS

Calvary Monument

Jean Bartlett photo

The Calvary Monument, Section H

By 1880, owners of residential property in San Francisco wanted the city's cemeteries removed. There just simply was not enough room for the dead. On August 1, 1901, the Board of Supervisors passed an ordinance which "prohibited burials within the city of San Francisco, and forbade the sale of cemetery lots to Odd Fellows, Masonic, Laurel Hill and Calvary cemeteries." In 1913, the Board of Supervisors passed an ordinance closing the old cemeteries and providing for the removal of bodies interred therein. Accompanied by his attorney, Mr. Garret McEnerny, Archbishop Patrick Riordan appeared before the Board to register a formal complaint protesting the closing of Mt. Calvary Cemetery. In 1937, the San Francisco Board of Supervisors passed ordinances ratified by the electorate at the November election, "Ordering and demanding the disinterring and removal of human bodies" from Mt. Calvary. In 1937, the Catholic Archdiocese ceased its opposition to disturbing Mt. Calvary Cemetery, and the removal process began on Monday, March 18, 1940. The Catholic Archdiocese of San Francisco oversaw the removal. A priest was in attendance at all phases of body removal and transport, and an inspector from the Department of Public Health was on hand for disinterment. Relatives could watch the disinterment if they wished. 120 lay personnel employed by Holy Cross did the actual work of exhuming and identifying remains at Mt. Calvary, and transporting them to Colma for reinternment within the Mt. Calvary mound area of Section H. The total number of burials in Mt. Calvary between 1860, and including the last two internments on October 18, 1909 of John McKenna and of Sister Fitzgerald, was 58,311. Of these, 39,307 were not claimed by relatives and were reinterred at Holy Cross.

Confederate Memorial Bench, Section H

On April 29, 2006, the Sons of Confederate Veterans dedicated a memorial bench for Brig. Gen. Edward Higgins, 1st Louisiana Heavy Artillery Regiment, 21st Louisiana Infantry and 22nd Louisiana Artillery, and Col. George Flournoy, Commander, 16th TX Infantry Regiment. Both officers were buried at Calvary Cemetery in San Francisco and moved to the Calvary Section at Holy Cross.

The Relief of the Last Supper at the Priest Plot, Section J

In the Priest Plot at Holy Cross, where over 300 priests are buried, the tombstones look towards a replica of Leonardo da Vinci's "Last Supper." The detailed artist's rendering, comforting all who visit this quiet patch of green, was meant to be owned by someone else, somewhere else. Cracked straight down the mid-

Jean Bartlett photo

Relief of the Last Supper at the Priest Plot

dle during transportation to its original buyer, the shipping company was told to dispose of it. They contacted Holy Cross. Would the Cemetery like to have a look? As it turned out, the crack did not touch any of the faces and was easily repaired – and so the white stone relief found a home at Holy Cross. On the back of the memorial is inscribed: "You Are A Priest Forever."

The Statue of Saint Francis, the Prince of Peace by Benny Bufano, Section W

During his lifetime (1898-1970), world-renowned Italian-born sculptor Benny Bufano would be both hailed and dismissed by art critics. Some considered his colossal sculptures to be the greatest thing that ever happened to the world of the modern sculpture. Others thought them too cute and/or too big to be taken seriously. In San Francisco, his long-time adopted city, Bufano

Jean Bartlett photo

Statue of St. Francis, the Prince of Peace by Benny Bufano

often battled these opposing points of views with city officials. Among Bufano's best known San Francisco works are numerous depictions of the city's patron saint, St. Francis of Assisi. In the 1920s, following a verbal agreement, Bufano created an 18-foot, 12.5-ton statue of St. Francis. The artist envisioned his St. Francis looking out over Twin Peaks, not unlike the landmark 98-foot statue of Christ the Redeemer looking out over Rio de Janeiro (Brazil). Bufano built his statue in an open field in France and it was exhibited in Paris to wildly enthusiastic reviews. San Francisco city officials didn't like it. They wouldn't even accept it when Bufano offered to give it to them for free. They didn't want to pay shipping charges. In 1955, the statue was brought to San Francisco where it found several homes before famed union leader Harry Bridges had it placed a few yards from the Longshoremen's Memorial Building at Fisherman's Wharf. The "Prince of Peace" statue at Holy Cross is Bufano's own miniature, colorful copy of the sculpture that had such a hard time finding a home. In his will, he left instructions that it was to be used as his grave marker. Bufano is buried in Section W, beneath his "Prince of Peace," in the field dedicated to infants lost at birth.

The Tomb of Reverend John P. Tobin, Section A

Father Tobin devoted his life to ministering to the poor and his instructions were that upon his death, a statue be erected to the indigent buried in "Potter's Field" at Holy Cross. He asked that

Jean Bartlett photo

Tomb of Reverend John P. Tobin

he too be buried with his "dear friends." His statue bears the words of John 11:25 "I am the resurrection and the life; whoever believes in me, even if he dies, will live." The marble statue by LeBreton was dedicated by the St. Vincent de Paul Society in 1929. Father Tobin is interred in front of the statue, at this "burying place for strangers." The Catholic Church, as a Corporal Work of Mercy, buries all Her beloved deceased in a caring and dignified manner.

Jean Bartlett photo

GRAVE
SYMBOLS

Jean Bartlett photo

Commonly used memorial symbols (traditional meanings):

Anchor – steadfast hope

Angels – messengers between God and man

Birds – the soul

Bunch of grapes and ear of corn – blood and body of Christ

Cherub – divine, wisdom or justice

Circle – perfection and eternity

Cross – Christ's suffering, belief in Christianity, death

Cross, crown and palm – trials, victory and reward
Crown – reward and glory
Dove – spirit of God, the Holy Spirit
Eight pointed star – regeneration
Fruit and vine – personality of Jesus Christ
Gate – passage from one realm to the next
Gourds – deliverance from grief
Holy Bible, open book – perfect intelligence and acceptance of Christianity
Hour glass – time and its flight
IHS – Jesus, Savior of men
INRI – (Latin) "Jesus the Nazarene, King of the Jews"
Ivy – faithfulness, memory and friendship
Lamb – infants, children, innocence
Laurel – victory and glory
Lily – purity and resurrection
Mermaid – dualism of Christ who is both God and man
Nine pointed star – fruits of the Holy Spirit, love, joy, suffering, gentleness, goodness, faith, meekness and temperance
Oak – strength
Palms – victory and martyrdom
Passion vine – crowning event in the life of Christ
Peacock – eternal life
Poppy – sleep, hence of death, since death is sleep
Rooster – man's fall from grace and his resurrection
Rose – red: martyrdom, white: purity
Shell – birth and resurrection
Six pointed star – the creator
Square – earth and life
Triangle – truth, equality and trinity
Weeping willow tree – the gospel of Christ

The meaning of color:

White – purity
Red – divine love
Violet – suffering love
Yellow – goodness of God
Grey – penance
Black and white – humility
Blue – truth and constancy
Green – hope and victory

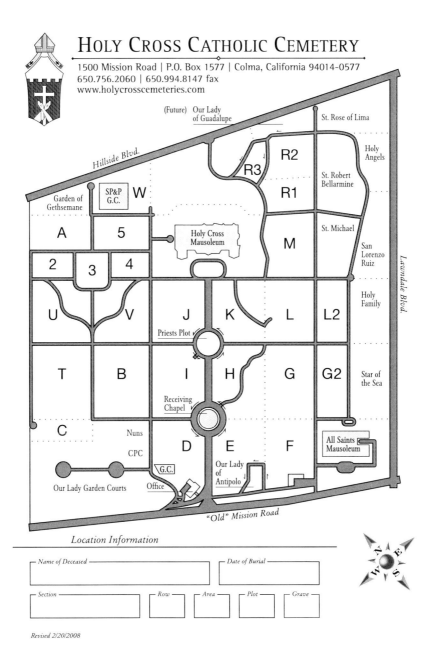

HOLY CROSS CATHOLIC CEMETERY

1500 Mission Road | P.O. Box 1577 | Colma, California 94014-0577
650.756.2060 | 650.994.8147 fax
www.holycrosscemeteries.com

(Future) Our Lady of Guadalupe

St. Rose of Lima

Hillside Blvd.

R2

R3

Holy Angels

St. Robert Bellarmine

R1

Garden of Gethsemane

SP&P G.C.

W

A

5

Holy Cross Mausoleum

M

St. Michael

San Lorenzo Ruiz

Lavendale Blvd.

2

3

4

U

V

J

K

L

L2

Holy Family

Priests Plot

T

B

I

H

G

G2

Star of the Sea

Receiving Chapel

C

Nuns

CPC

D

E

F

All Saints Mausoleum

Our Lady Garden Courts

G.C.

Office

Our Lady of Antipolo

"Old" Mission Road

Location Information

Name of Deceased

Date of Burial

Section

Row

Area

Plot

Grave

N E S W

Revised 2/20/2008

Jean Bartlett photo

THE WOMEN
BEHIND THIS BOOK

About the Author •

Born in San Francisco, **Jean Bartlett** has worked as the Arts and Features Correspondent for the *Pacifica Tribune* for the past 13 years and continuing. She is additionally the Arts and Features Writer for the *Peninsula Progress*. Along with these papers, she has written for such print and online media as the *San Jose Mercury*, the *Oakland Tribune*, the *San Mateo Times* and *Bay Area Business Woman*. A family history biographer, she writes individual histories for both private clients and memorial websites such as *Making Everlasting Memories*. The author of the award-winning children's book *IndiAsia and the Dragon*, Ms. Bartlett has additionally written theater for American Conservatory Theater's Young Conservatory, the Barefoot Play Readers Repertory Theatre Company and the Pacifica School District. Her online website, *Jean's Magazines*, provides press (in-depth interviews and reviews) for artists and musicians. She is the scriptwriter behind the online, *Quip Films by Bartlett*. Additionally she has written for Hallmark Cards, Inc. and worked as a Bay Area lyricist/melody writer. Her grandparents are interred at Holy Cross.

About the Director of Cemeteries, Holy Cross

Monica J. Williams is the Director of Cemeteries for the Archdiocese of San Francisco and considers it a special privilege to oversee Holy Cross Cemetery in Colma, where five generations of her family are buried. Raised in the Sunset District of San Francisco, she attended St. Cecilia Grammar School and St. Rose Academy, and graduated Phi Beta Kappa from The Catholic University of America in Washington, DC. Ms Williams began working in Funeral Service in 1989 and is licensed in California as a Funeral Director and Cemetery Manager. She represents the Archdiocese in the Catholic Cemetery Conference and Catholic Cemeteries of the West. Her love of history has motivated her to create a number of walking tours for the cemetery and research the many stories honored here. Ms. Williams resides in San Francisco, where she volunteers her time at St. Gabriel Parish. She is the doting Auntie to the World's Cutest Nieces: Katie, Emily and Ella.

About the Family Services Manager, Holy Cross

Christine Stinson, Family Services Manager, has an extensive and unique background in funeral and cemetery practice. Since 1987, she has served Holy Cross first as a Family Services Counselor then as Family Services Manager. She was co-owner of Stinson Funeral Home in Pennsylvania and currently is co-owner of Colma Cremation and Funeral Services. She is co-creator of Good Grief Radio and co-founder of the Good Grief Store. She is a Nationally Certified Bereavement Facilitator, a member of the American Academy of Bereavement and a member of the National Catholic Ministry to the Bereaved. She is co-creator of "Healthy Grief Support." She is the facilitator for the 125th Anniversary Celebration for Holy Cross Catholic Cemetery including the publishing of the "Cookbook of Memories" and this book, "125 Years of History, Ministry and Service". With her experience, her talent to adapt to the changes in funeral and cemetery practices, grief education and as a victim of suicide, Ms. Stinson brings an in-depth understanding and ability to meet the individual needs and provide caring support to the families of Holy Cross.

Holy Cross photo

Mourners arrive by streetcar to Holy Cross